Having worked with thousands of people this book is highly relevant. As a Therapist touched by addiction, I help people find build a life they love. In almost all of these situations digital intrusion is impacting how we form and maintain intimate relationships, and live our lives on purpose. The digital device has become a tool of enslavement. This book is a call to everyone who wants to be free. Take the reins.

Todd Davis, PhD, LADC
EmergingStrength.com

As a parent of two young children and an educator of students in middle school, I found Christina's book to be enlightening, constructive and thought-provoking, especially as it comes from a biblical perspective. Rearing and educating children in the year 2021 comes with many challenges in uncharted territory. This book helped me to understand why many children engage and react to situations in the way that they do and provided me with the tools needed to appropriately react. As an educator, I need to be aware of the newest ways technology can positively and negatively impact students and was glad when I came across this resource guide. This book opens doors for conversations about the importance of using technology not only appropriately, but safely. It provides the reader with many references and at the end of each chapter allows the opportunity for discussion, as there are many engaging questions asked.

Erica L. Higginbotham, M.Ed.

Christina Avallone's book is an exciting new addition to conversations about technology and parenting. Parents who are eager to respond to the challenges our rapidly accelerating digital technologies are presenting for children's lives would benefit greatly from reading. The book is thoughtful and relatable, and it makes an excellent resource for introducing some of the most pressing concerns about technology in our time. Beyond its commentary on some of today's technological problems, the book is filled with discussion questions that make it an excellent option for parent groups who want to grow together in learning how to care for their children.

In 2007 the iPhone was introduced and the method of human communication and unfettered and nearly immediate access to information in Industrial countries was dramatically changed forever. Some may argue for the better and others for the worse. Christina has done an exceptional job of identifying where "by the speed of light" the advancement of technology and its penetration into our lives and well-being can be detrimental if we permit it. I picked up this book as a parent of two young adults expecting to gain insight into how technology has impacted their lives only to read and be convicted how technology has impacted me as a 50 something-year-old. This book goes beyond identifying the negative impact technology can have on us individually and on our culture by providing practical and more importantly biblical insight into how to have the benefit of technology while limiting the potentially negative side effects. In my opinion it is worth everyone's time and especially the time of those who are parenting or interacting regularly with teenagers and those younger individuals to read this book.

Mike Wiethorn
Husband, Father, Practicing Attorney

Since reading Christina's book, I don't check my phone as soon as I wake up, and I bought an alarm clock! I now wake with more creative thoughts that aren't lost as they were when I grabbed my cell phone first thing in the morning. A new habit for me is to keep my cell phone in a separate room while at home, or in my purse when out with others. If I have put mine away first, I notice now that friends put their cell phones away without my having to ask. I want to lead by example with family and friends. I want the change to start with me and spread to others without words or pressure. My new habits with digital engagement have allowed more room for good things in my life, and I enjoy sharing those good things when asked. This book gave me real perspective on how our cell phones are impacting our lives, and what needs to be done to get our lives back.

Lori Mateer
Mother of three grown children

When my children were younger, I bounced like a yoyo between no limits and being too strict with their phone usage. The problem grew worse, and then I discovered Christina's book. She provides candid truth and practical tips for helping families successfully navigate today's technical tidal wave. No matter what stage you find yourself in your parenting walk, using Christina's balanced approach will reduce conflict, strengthen boundaries, and give you peace of mind. This is a must read for every parent, grandparent, and teacher!

S. Michael Streib
Father of four, grandfather and retired law professor

THRIVING
IN A
DIGITAL WORLD

A Workable Plan For Taking Back the Reins Of Your Family

CHRISTINA AVALLONE

WESTBOW
PRESS®
A DIVISION OF THOMAS NELSON
& ZONDERVAN

WestBow Press books may be ordered through booksellers or by contacting:

WestBow Press
A Division of Thomas Nelson & Zondervan
1663 Liberty Drive
Bloomington, IN 47403
www.westbowpress.com
844-714-3454

Manuscript assistance provided by Dr. Dori Anne Abbott

"Are You Addicted to Your Phone?" taken from the September 2017 issue of *Brio* magazine
published by Focus on the Family. © 2017 Focus on the Family. Used with permission.

All Scripture quotations are taken from The Holy Bible, New International
Version®, NIV® Copyright © 1973, 1978, 1984, 2011 by Biblica,
Inc.® Used by permission. All rights reserved worldwide.

ISBN: 978-1-6642-2096-6 (sc)
ISBN: 978-1-6642-2097-3 (hc)
ISBN: 978-1-6642-2095-9 (e)

Library of Congress Control Number: 2021901246

Printed in the United States of America.

WestBow Press rev. date: 04/02/2021

CONTENTS

Acknowledgements

Most importantly I want to praise my Abba Father for never giving up on me, chasing me down and inviting me in when I least deserved it. I cannot thank Him enough.

I want to thank my husband Marc for putting up with all my quirkiness. God gave me you in 1986, our senior year of high school, for which I am forever grateful. Your words of encouragement always inspire me to be a better person. I would not be who I am without you.

To my 2 wonderful daughters Jessica and Samantha, I would not be the mom I am without having been your mom. There are many things I wish I could do over, but those moments have made us who we are today. I am so proud of you both. Your willingness to come alongside me in writing my book meant the world to me. Your valuable input helped formulate the book to where it is today.

I want to thank Kelley Streib because without her there would be no book, she was my inspiration. I remember Kelley cheering me on after a "Parenting in a Digital World" small group class planting the seed to write a book to help parents Thrive. Sometimes I need the encouraging words to get me going, thanks Kelley.

I want to thank Victory Family Church for hosting the "Parenting in a Digital World" event and small group. Many thoughts and ideas from these events have flowed into my book.

I want to thank Dori Anne for all her tireless assistance she provided. This manuscript would not be what it is today without her help.

I want to thank all the countless people who have spurred me on, prayed with or for me especially when I needed it the most. I could not have completed this manuscript without each one of you.

This book is dedicated to all those in the fray; those taking responsibility for the well-being of their families; those standing up against the overwhelming forces of digital saturation and surveillance capitalism. Keep on keeping on, and you will thrive!

FOREWORD

In today's world, it can often feel as though technology is running rampant over our lives and the lives of our children. Technology has now become a necessity in the workforce, our educational systems, our personal lives—and even in the church. This makes finding balance in the use of screens even more challenging, especially for our children.

As parents endeavoring to raise Godly children, how do we protect them from the harmful websites and apps to which they have access? How do we engage our children in other ways, so that their time is not consumed with video games and digital platforms? We are called to train our children in *the way they should go*, and this starts with informing ourselves. *Parenting in a Digital World* offers parents practical tools to help families navigate life in the twenty-first century, as well as ways to develop deeper relationships with each other and with Christ.

Having hosted *Parenting in a Digital World* conferences for Christina Avallone, I believe the data she has compiled over the years for this book, coupled with wisdom from the Scriptures, provides much-needed wisdom and information for parents as they train and teach their children to walk with Christ and not succumb to traps set before them.

Pastor John Nuzzo
Lead Pastor
Victory Family Church

INTRODUCTION

When my children were young, I thought I would not survive due to sleep deprivation and its twin sister utter exhaustion. At that time, I started writing a book called, *Sleep Deprivation: You Will Survive! A Mother's Story*. Recently I read this book attempt of mine and found it funny. Apparently, I was too tired to continue because I never made it past page ten. Fast forward 21 years and I have seen changes in child rearing and family life that give me pause, make me say, *Huh*, and cause me to wonder what today's kids will be like in just a few, short years if parents don't take back the reins of family life. We know that whoever or whatever captures a child's heart controls the trajectory of his affections, thoughts, emotions, and behaviors on up into adult life. Ideally, in God's economy that should be the parents. Sadly, that is not always the way it turns out.

The essential landscape of how we rear our children has changed. I used to talk with my kids when they were in their strollers. We would play together with chalk, Play-Doh, finger paints and crayons. Children played outside with other children *in real life!* Now I see parents on their phones and the kids are playing by themselves or worse yet, playing on an electronic device/tablet while being pushed in the stroller. Those same children can be seen at restaurants at the dinner table, still glued to the same electronic device. This concerns me for several reasons, and if you picked up this book, I have a feeling that it concerns you as well.

Many parents have expressed to me how much they hate the amount of time their children spend on video games, watching YouTube offerings, making TikTok videos, scrolling through Facebook and Instagram, and generally living "out there" in the cyberworld while their bodies are parked at home. Are they actually safe at home if their minds and hearts are "somewhere out there?" What changes are occurring in their not-yet-developed brains from spending so much time gazing at a screen?

We know it's not possible to eliminate electronic entertainment, or keep our kids sequestered from it, but shouldn't we at least have a plan to manage it? Where are the guidelines that teach us to do that? These are questions I am asking, and they are questions that millions of parents are asking right now. Back in the 1950s and 1960s, parents had Dr. Spock, an American pediatrician whose book, *Baby and Child Care* was one of the best-selling tomes in history. He answered basic questions that parents had with simple instructions and guidelines to promote the development of healthy children. Today we don't have a Dr. Spock, so I am stepping up to the plate to share what I have learned. I don't have all the answers, but I do have *some*.

I have long felt a burden to share how we can parent differently, how we can take back the reins of our children's hearts. Before you put this book down because you don't want to hear all the negative messages about what your kids are into, understand that I am writing this book as a message of HOPE not condemnation. I do not want to see our kids growing up begging for their parents' attention, because we are too busy. Here's what I know:

- I know when the kids hit the teenage years, if the parents *now* want to hold a conversation, it is too late if they never established a relationship with their children. Teenagers no longer care, nor do they want our attention.
- I know that dinnertime can and should be a sacred place, where conversations are held, topics discussed, problems solved, feelings are sorted out. This is no longer happening. We need to change that, and you will find out the reasons *why* in this book.
- I know that where your treasure is, there also is your heart and your affections. Since time is our greatest treasure, whatever we or our children spend the most time pursuing is the thing that has captured our hearts.
- I know that parents have much more power than they think they do. We've been conditioned by the world around us to believe that we have few rights and that our children have all the power.

Indeed, with the whining and crying to be like everyone else, it's hard to believe they don't. But the reality is, parents can and should direct and manage the lives of their children with the ultimate goal of their becoming perfect (whole, complete, lacking nothing) adults.

In this book you will gain insight into how to balance technology with everyday living. You will be reminded that you not only *can* take the reins back, but that you have a God-given mandate (overwhelming authority) to do so. You will be armed not only with the statistics but also the tools to keep your child from becoming yet another statistic. You will learn how to "keep calm and carry on" by managing technology before it manages your family.

ONE

IN THE BLINK OF AN EYE:
WHAT'S A PARENT TO DO?

"In the blink of an eye, everything can change."
Zig Ziglar

In what seemed like the blink of an eye, our entire society changed from wall-mounted phones in our homes to clunky car phones permanently attached to the floorboards to rudimentary handheld phones and then to smartphones. This technology has been 150 years in the making. The first cell phone technology appeared in 1843 when a chemist named Michael Faraday began his research to see if electricity could be conducted in space.[1] Today 94 percent of Americans have and use a cellular telephone. On average, we check them 150 times per day! This number equates to every six minutes during our waking hours, or every ten minutes during any given 24-hour period! The obvious question raised by these numbers is when are kids sleeping? How much and how well? While we sleep 68 percent of us have them next to our heads. We send more than six million text messages every day - 90 percent of those text messages are read within three minutes of receiving them.[2]

We could draw many conclusions from these statistics and raise even more questions that demand answers. Such as, What are the people doing at the time that they immediately answer those text messages? Are they driving? Conversing with others? In school? At work? In church? How distracted is the average person if he is checking his phone 150 times during the day? Does this qualify as obsession? Or is it merely efficiency? What are the long-term physical and cognitive effects of being tethered to and dependent on our phones? The one thing we do know, and can all agree on, is that this technology is here to stay. Like all other technology, it is not inherently evil or good—it is merely a tool to accomplish something the means to an end.

So what was the end in mind? Connection. The cell phone has revolutionized the way we communicate with one another, but as a grand social experiment it remains to be seen whether we are truly becoming more connected. The argument could be made either way. Originally, this technology was merely a way to keep a very mobile society connected to one another and untethered to a stationary phone. But with the advent of the smartphone, users now browse the internet, check social media, store hundreds of phone numbers they will never remember by heart, and keep scores of books they will likely never read. These devices are millions of times more powerful than the missile guidance system that put the first man on the moon just a few short decades ago.

> **You wouldn't be wrong in saying an iPhone could be used to guide 120,000,000 Apollo era spacecraft to the moon, all at the same time.**[3]

What is a parent or other adult to do with this powerful tool? I mean all our *other* power tools are under lock and key - or else put up where the kids can't get to them. Yet every day we see this powerful tool in the hands of toddlers. So what is a parent to do? How can we survive this change that seemed to happen in the blink of an eye? Where are the rules and guidelines to help us navigate the societal changes that have come as a result of our tech-obsessed world? And maybe the most important question of all is, How can we not only *survive,* but also *thrive* during this time of catastrophic change?

First, parents can acknowledge that there is no standard out there. If I were to ask ten mothers and fathers how much time for a child is too much to play a video game, I would likely get at least ten different answers! If I were to ask a pediatrician how much sleep my child should be getting, she would give me an exact number of hours based my child's age. But if I were to ask that same doctor how many hours are considered acceptable for my child to kill zombies online, I'm fairly confident I wouldn't get a sure and ready answer. This professional with thousands of hours of schooling and practice doesn't know for sure. She can give you her opinion, or what other "experts" say, but to date there has been no real guideline handed out to parents. That's because we are in a sort of grand social experiment. Until an entire generation that has grown up from the cradle holding a cell phone or a game controller in their hands, we won't know some of the far reaching and indelible effects of allowing them unfettered access to this kind of power.

> *Without a map in hand, the treasure cannot be found.*
> *No one can draw a map to a place they haven't been.*[4]

I remember once pulling into a parking lot, hopping out of the car, and turning around to discover that I had parked horribly crooked! I wasn't even inside the lines! How did this happen? I'm a good driver, but I used the car next to me as a guide for my parking. Because that driver was parked poorly, so was I. When it comes to navigating digital devices and technology with our families, it's easy to do the same thing. We base our decisions on what other families are doing—regardless of whether they have "parked straight" or not! Some influential writers have outlined their standards (parking lines) for successful family life.

God's Word is the final word. It teaches us that time and attention are the currency of relationships—make sure you are giving each family member enough of each! Unconditional love combined with high expectations is a recipe for success with children. Love them for *who they are,* but expect their behavior to stay within the parking lines. At the end of the day, the success of a family is not measured by the size of the house, the cost of the toys, the grades in school, or the size of the paychecks. True success in a family is determined by the quality of the relationships within it. Long after the parents are gone, sons and daughters will live on in some sort of relationship with one another. Best to build those relationships on a sure foundation.[5]

Choosing faith over fear is acknowledging what physics (the Puli exclusion principle) has taught us—that two objects cannot occupy the same space at the same time. Faith and fear can't coexist in our family life—one will always win out. Make sure the winner is faith! Although it can seem overwhelming to take on the challenge of digital intrusion and addiction, you can do it by God's grace and your diligent effort. Together you and God make a majority!

It's important for readers to know that I am not some Luddite[6] who is railing against the reality of technology. I am first and foremost a mom of two beautiful, grown daughters. Like some kind of real life Forrest Gump, I have lived and parented through some of the most significant technological changes in the history of the world. Think back to the year 2000 if you can. Rarely anyone had a cellular phone. Walkie-talkie type phones from Nextel and pagers were much more the norm, and still not ubiquitous. Children still played freely outside. When inside, they perhaps watched VHS movies. Cable television was just coming into its own, while today cable subscriptions have been chucked by millions of families in favor of other streaming services and devices. Play-Doh, crayons, gel pens, and markers were necessary supplies. The tragedy of the attacks of September 11 had not yet stolen the innocence and trust of Americans, and the horror of the Columbine shootings (1999) seemed like an outlier, an anomaly, something that surely wouldn't be repeated regularly. It's easy to see in hindsight why parents began feeling safer with their children indoors, but this safety was and still is an illusion. I wonder, how safe can children be when we are bringing *who knows what* inside the house, inside their bedrooms, inside their minds and hearts?

Because I chose to leave a successful, corporate career and stay at home with my children, I saw the necessity of bringing the same discipline and order I had used to manage a million dollar a week 401K plan for the Vanguard Group to the job of family management. My husband traveled a lot for his job at this time, so for at least 50 percent of the time, I was carrying this task alone. Organizational skills, rules, boundaries, and guidelines became even more necessary to make sure that nothing fell through the cracks—most importantly not my children! And still, as they grew, I made mistakes. When my daughter was 15, I bought her a smart phone thinking that I was being a great mom. I had no idea the depression, anxiety, and stress she would suffer from the peer pressure of social media, cyberbullying, FOMO (fear of missing out), and the dings to her self-confidence when she mysteriously didn't get the number of "likes" she thought she was due. I quickly realized that this was a recipe for disaster.

So, I began teaching a class called, "Parenting in a Digital World." We had an event to introduce it that drew more than 550 parents, grandparents, teachers, and friends, all concerned about the same issues that I was—the influence of this technology on the young people they loved and how to draw up and implement a reasonable, workable solution to it. Over many semesters this class has continued to draw crowds of folks who come in broken and left empowered and encouraged! If our children are priceless gifts from God, then caring for them—helping them not only survive the onslaught of technology but thrive in it—should be job #1. Sitting around bemoaning the fate of an entire generation addicted to the "pings" of social media notifications and the dopamine rush that accompanies video gaming isn't enough. We need an actionable plan, and the grace and strength of character combined with the will to carry out that plan.

For a minute let's talk about the difference between desires, dreams, plans, and goals. When our children are born, we dream BIG dreams for them! We dream that they will be smart, funny, accomplished, kind, beautiful, well-favored by others, lucky in love, successful in business endeavors, responsible, independent, and hopefully grateful for our sacrifices on their behalf. We dream that they will change the world in a positive way and bring honor to God, blessings to others, and pride to us as parents. These dreams exist exclusively in our minds because that is the domain of dreams. In order to have a goal, these dreams must be accompanied by a plan. The clearer and more specific the plan, the more workable is the goal, and the more likely the dream is to be realized.

A goal cannot be accomplished if certain elements are beyond our control. For instance, it would be unwise to have as a goal that your spouse will appreciate your efforts in the home. Why is this an unworkable goal? Because it involves the free will of another person. You cannot control the elements of this, so it can be a dream or a desire, but not a goal. Likewise, once your children are nearing the age of 18, you cannot start here with the goal of them wisely managing their use of technology. They are now too independent (and rightfully so) to control all the factors. This goal and this plan must start when you still have a modicum of control in the home. Of course, some parents have abdicated this control from the start, but hopefully you do not fall into this category. If you do, it's never too late! There is hope! You didn't know what you didn't know, but now you do! Start now. Start today. There is no time like the present. As long as that child is under your influence, you can and should be using that influence for their protection and good.

Managing anything—kids, schedules, technology, money, physical fitness, etc.—is a multifactorial process. For instance, physical fitness is comprised of four components: balance, strength, endurance, and flexibility. All must be addressed to achieve true fitness. Managing your family's "digital footprint" is no different. You must have not only a dream, but also realistic and achievable goals that are fleshed out with workable, flexible, reasonable plans. With that in mind, this book will concern itself with the *misuse and overuse* of technology, not the concept or beneficial use of it. But let us talk for a moment about power, shall we? Let's dig into the concepts of authority, power, coercion, and seduction. With the explosion of technology in homes and schools, a shift occurred in the hierarchy of power and influence. Because authority, power, coercion, and seduction are all methods for capturing the human heart, these are important concepts for any discussion on parents, children, or tools and technology for that matter!

Authority

Regarding parenting, the best definition of authority is the right to give orders, make decisions, and enforce obedience. Children learn to listen to and obey God by first listening to and obeying their parents. Two questions that should be asked at this juncture are, *who is in charge of your home?* And *who should be?* Sadly, the answer to these questions isn't always the same. Authority has been passed down from God as the means to accomplishing His purposes on earth. The concept of another making decisions and wielding authority is not a popular one. From the Garden of Eden where Satan challenged Adam and Eve with, *Did God really say...?*[7] to modern times where we are sometimes too lenient because others have abused their authority in our lives, most humans (small or large) chafe at the exercise of authority. God has given parents, grandparents, and teachers authority so they can bring children the greatest amount of good while protecting them from the greatest amount of harm. The right to exercise parental authority comes directly from God. If you have a blended family, this can be tricky. We've all seen "that kid" who shouts at his stepfather, "You're not my dad!" If you have taken on the role of parenting someone else's biological child, make no mistake—you are still exercising godly authority for their good.

Power

There exist two kinds of power: overt power and covert power—brute strength and subtle influence. I once heard a preacher extol the importance of women as "the neck" of the family. The husband may be the head, but it never turns without the neck directing it! In this book we will talk extensively about the influential power that parents, teachers, coaches and extended family members like grandparents, aunts, uncles, and older siblings exert on children. Influence is the greatest kind of power, though it doesn't get a lot of fanfare. It is quiet, subtle, but powerful! One thing we don't often think about is that we will be held accountable for how we used our influence in this life. Did we exert and leverage our influence for good? Or did we remain neutral to "keep peace" in the family? Someday we will have to answer for those choices.

Coercion

The online experience for children and teens depends on psychological coercion. In a coercive environment, the victim adapts to a series of baby steps—each step is so small that the victim doesn't notice the changes to his beliefs or behaviors.[8] Psychological coercion is at the core of peer pressure, but it's also at the core of the online world. By shouting the accepted narrative long enough, loud enough, and often enough, television, movies, "news" outlets, and social media sites push the digital consumer into a lockstep belief system from which he cannot escape. Psychological coercion overtakes our critical thinking abilities and our God-given free will. One way this is done is by the rejection of alternate information and opinions that differ with the ruling narrative.

As an example, most young Americans if asked what is causing the worsening of wildfires on the West Coast would answer, "global warming." There is no room for alternate reality or facts such as the persuasion and pressure of environmentalists to stop controlled burning of forests, or the mismanagement of utility companies. Not practicing controlled burns creates a situation where there is much more fuel available when a spark ignites the landscape, and keeping towers on power lines built in the 1920s is a prime ingredient with seasonal drought and high winds for massive blazes like the Camp fire.[9] This is one simple example, and we as adults who learned reasoning skills in our youth ("question everything!") can handle it. But think about the impressionable children who are baby stepped along the road of thinking that is completely antithetical to your family's values. This is nothing more than psychological coercion—the frog boiling in a pot of water whose temperature has been raised one degree at a time. Poor frog doesn't even know he's boiling until it's too late.

Seduction

One of the dictionary definitions of a seduction is *something that attracts or charms.* Electronic seduction is real, and it has a hold on the hearts of our children. Marketing is by nature seductive. From the 1960s commercials for mouthwash to the pop-up ads on the internet, consumers are swayed to spend time and money for goods, services, and entertainment they don't really need. When movies feature cool characters smoking, tobacco sales go up among young people.[10] Video games are a multi-billion dollar industry advertised on television, before YouTube videos, at sporting events, and even before movie trailers at local theaters.[11] Television shows are hyped during commercial breaks between other television shows. Movies are marketed during the previews before the main feature a year before they are released. The seduction is constant and it's convincing.

Many scholars agree that the internet plays an important role in the seduction of young minds to radical causes.[12] No matter which side of the aisle you vote for, radicalization of young impressionable minds is dangerous. It leads to bigotry, lone-wolf behaviors, domestic terrorism, and states of rage. It feeds the idols of the heart. For those who are neurologically sensitive, the seduction of fringe radicalism feeds into their fears, suspicions, and rage. When we think of seduction, we generally think of it in sexual terms, but the essence of seduction is an appeal to our basic human desires of power, prestige, popularity, peace, security, belonging, respect, position of dominance, and ultimately meaning.

Questions to Ponder & Discuss

1. How many times a day do you think you check your phone?
2. Do you think that is too much, not enough or just right?
3. Where do you store your phone at bedtime?
4. Where is your child's phone at bedtime?
5. Why could your phone in the bedroom be a problem?
6. If asked, would others see you as engaged or distracted because of your phone? How?
7. Do you ever feel you missed the boat, that you are in over your head with technology in regard to yourself and/or your children? Why?
8. What steps have you taken to protect yourself/your family with overuse/misuse of technology?

TWO

ARE YOU ADDICTED?
AND WHY IT MATTERS

*"The most familiar behaviors that are resistant to change
are those that involve addiction of some sort…"*
Gordon Livingston, M.D.

Are You Addicted to Your Phone?

Have you ever – Yes or No *from Focus on the Family*

- Been accused of being addicted to your cell phone?
- Argued with someone about how much you use your cell phone?
- Left your phone face up on the dinner table or right beside you?
- Secretly tried to check your phone under the table at a client meeting or in a conference room?
- Left your house without your phone & went back to get it?
- Forgot your phone at home and asked someone to bring it to you?
- Slept with your phone under your pillow or in bed with you?
- Read a text or texted while having a real-life conversation?
- Interrupted a conversation by laughing at a text?
- Texted while walking?
- Texted while driving?
- Checked social media sites multiple times an hour?
- Gotten really mad when your phone didn't get service?

- Fallen asleep while texting?
- Always kept your cell phone charger with you ?
- Panicked when your battery ran out and you didn't have a charger?
- Downloaded so many apps and pictures that you no longer have storage space on your phone?
- Gotten angry if asked to turn off your phone or put it away?

What did you think of the quiz? Did it make you laugh, mad, angry, frustrated, think of someone else? Whenever I have a speaking engagement, I start with this quiz. When everyone is done with the quiz, their reactions run the gamut of emotions. As they are pondering their responses, I take out a plastic bag of white powder, get out my mirror, put the powder on the mirror, take my credit card and cut the powder (as I have seen on TV) then I roll a dollar bill and go to snort the powder. By now, I have oohs and ahhs from the crowd and even hear, "Is she really doing what I think she is doing?" As I am about to snort the powder I stop suddenly, hold up my phone and ask, "How many of you have given a phone to your child?"

The unthinkable question is next, how many of us would give our children an opioid or cocaine? Everyone's head is shaking *no*, some with disgust. However, if you have given your child a phone, what is happening in his brain with the addiction to his phone, is the same thing that happens when his brain is responding to an addictive drug. There are also similarities between cell phone overuse and behavioral addictions like compulsive gambling. Some of them include:

- Loss of control over the behavior
- Persistence: having difficulty limiting the behavior
- Tolerance: the need to engage in the behavior more often to get the same feeling
- Severe negative consequences stemming from the behavior (i.e. being "grounded")
- Withdrawal: feelings of irritability and anxiety when the behavior isn't practiced
- Relapse: picking up the habit again after periods of avoidance[13]

What is addiction?

We joke about being "addicted" to chocolate, to our phones, or to other people, but what do we mean when we talk about addiction? According to the American Psychiatric Association, addiction is a "complex condition, a brain disease that is manifested by compulsive substance use despite harmful consequence."[14] Let's unpack that for a minute. If you have ever argued with your child about turning off a video game or giving up his phone for a period of time (maybe even a short dinner), you have seen compulsive behavior at work. If you have had to threaten that child or teen to comply, you have seen compulsivity at work. If your child has stayed in the bathroom longer than necessary so they could finish looking at or playing on a phone, or if they have stayed up past a healthy bedtime while looking at their phone, if they have "sneak peeked" to see if they got a text or dm (direct message) during a class, staff meeting, or sermon (!) you have seen compulsivity at work. What creates this compulsive behavior? Why does a child risk getting "grounded" for five more minutes of game time?

All addictions—from gambling to drugs to technology are all based on the same underlying function. The brain expects that an activity will produce a reward. This reward may or may not be obvious to the addict. The lower parts of the brain interpret the activity as a positive experience even if that activity is dangerous, harmful, addictive, or even painful. For gamblers, it's not the possibility of winning that gives them the "high." It's the risk. Sadly, over time it takes more and more of a stimulus to produce the same level of reward. That is why alcoholics can literally drink themselves to death. The greater the risk, the more dopamine released in the brain and the more satisfaction to the addict. Research has shown that the act of checking emails, texts, and social media releases dopamine in the same way that gambling away large sums of money at the craps table does.[15]

Changes in the brain's wiring are what cause people to have intense cravings for (the substance or behavior) and make it hard to stop. It's truly NOT something to joke about. If we knew that someone or something was hijacking our child's brain—if we really believed that were happening, we would do WHATEVER it takes to stop it, wouldn't we? If our child were snorting cocaine, would we give her a "hit" just to keep her quiet in the car? Or at church? Or in the grocery store? That seems obnoxiously bold for me to say but stay with me for just a minute.

Dopamine Dings

No doubt you have heard of the neurotransmitter called *dopamine.* Your body makes it, and your neural system uses it to relay messages between cells. This is why it is called (as all neurotransmitters are) a chemical messenger. We hear a lot about dopamine these days from areas as diverse as Parkinson's research, addiction treatment, and ethical considerations of digital engagement. Dopamine specifically plays a role in motivation, pleasure, and satisfaction. When dopamine neurons become activated, they release dopamine. When something good happens to us (especially if it is unexpected), dopamine neurons are activated. Dopamine is the "feel-good" neurotransmitter. We get a boost when we eat foods we love, engage in sexual activity, drink alcohol, take drugs, engage in regular exercise, and (as I will explain more later), when we are playing video games or outcome-based games on our phones (i.e. Candy Crush, etc.) Ever wonder why your kids are so quiet while watching YouTube videos? Their dopamine is "dinging" and giving them deep, hedonistic pleasure. I probably don't need to tell you how ugly it can get when you try to take that source of pleasure away.

Dopamine has been implicated in schizophrenia and ADHD. This neurotransmitter causes us to want, to desire, to search and seek out pleasure. We eat a second piece of cake; we don't turn off a pornographic website popup immediately, we play games instead of reading, learning, or connecting in real life. People with high levels of dopamine—whether because of their innate brain wiring or because they are amped up on digital, dopamine "dings" (the sounds made when you score points, get an instant message, an Instagram "like," or any other of a number of alerts on your phone) are *sensation seekers.*[16] A lack of dopamine, or a dopamine deficiency has been implicated in certain conditions like Alzheimer's, depressive disorders, binge-eating, addiction, and gambling. These are important considerations not only because we want to keep our kids (and ourselves) addiction free, but they are also important because we will need a PLAN to keep dopamine levels from dropping too quickly when we take away or lessen the amount of the addictive substance (digital engagement). But make no mistake: we DO need to regulate this engagement, no matter how ugly it gets.

Race to the Bottom of the Brain Stem

Is it a coincidence that most of our opportunities for digital engagement come associated with bright colors, pleasant sounds, instant rewards (albeit of artificial currency like "gold coins"), and addictive formats? No, it is not a coincidence. Those tasked with creating digital games and activities know full well that dopamine causes humans to want, desire, seek out, and search. It increases our level of arousal and promotes goal-directed behavior.[17] It creates reward-seeking circuits or "loops" in the nervous system that make us repeat the pleasurable behavior—whether it is checking Instagram for "likes" or whether enjoying "sex, drugs, and rock n roll." It is all the same. Dopamine signals feedback for predicted rewards. If you have learned to associate a cue like a drink of alcohol or downing a big Mac with pleasure or with a lessening of angst or pain, then you will start getting increases in dopamine deep in the brain in response to merely *the sight* of those things. Your brain anticipates the coming reward—even if that reward is merely the cessation of stress or pain caused by the addictive substance itself.

*It's like a switch, clickin' off in my head. Turns
the hot light off and the cool one on,
and all of a sudden there's peace. — Tennessee
Williams, Cat on a Hot Tin Roof*

Former Google ethicist Tristan Harris has drawn a lot of attention because he was the first to shed light (back in 2017) on the addictive nature of social media. He has made headlines by calling for tech companies to "stop the downgrading of humans," by engineering the technology to create addiction and diminish our intellect.[18] He rightly claims that today's overuse of technology fits our "reptile brains" to a tee because that is what the games and apps are designed to do. They are designed to give us pleasure by tickling our dopamine receptors, creating the need for a return to that pleasurable behavior, and miring us in an addiction that is at best a waste of time, and at worst, destroying our humanity.

By "reptile brain" Harris means the brain stem—the part of the brain that is responsible for primitive survival instincts like rage, fear, and jealousy. It is composed of the brain stem, the cerebellum, and the basal ganglia. Collectively they are known as the "reptile brain" or the limbic system. This system is in charge of the stress response in humans (fight/flight/freeze). It would take another whole book to talk about the dangers of living with an elevated stress response—everything from brain shrinkage to belly fat to decreased immune function to digestive issues—but suffice it to say that having the stress response repeatedly activated artificially (no real tiger to fight) makes humans fat, sick, stupid, and tired.

If you have ever seen a child or teen after a few hours of playing video games or watching YouTube videos, you will notice a vacant, hollow look to their eyes; perhaps a flush of red in the face, neck, and/or ears; shallow breathing and a sheen of perspiration. They haven't actually engaged in a fight with a tiger, but their stress system has done mighty battle. They are in a full-blown stress response, and for the next four hours, their immunity to sickness will be diminished. Their digestive systems will be on standby, and their higher thinking will be diminished to survival strategies. This is not "normal" or natural—no matter what society says differently.

Human downgrading is a term that ethicists have come up with in response to problems experienced by modern man like information overload, addiction and overuse, burnout, polarization (as seen in political posts on social media), excess outrage, excess vanity (wanting "likes"), shortening attention spans and cynicism. These facets are all connected, and it is NOT an accident. They are all part of the race to capture human attention—the race for the bottom of the brain stem. The multi-billion-dollar gaming and social media industries would not be rich if they had to just get attention in a one-to-one fashion. Instead they use a sort of "crowdsourcing" to make us dependent on the likes and attention of others. By doing this, they can be assured that our phones will always be present, always be open, and we will always be looking, searching, seeking for that next pleasurable ding of dopamine. They capture us as adults (who should know better) and give us no moral leg to stand on when confronting our kids.

One must ask in the light of these ethical concerns why those who create and promote the use of technology don't allow their own children access to it? They consistently send their children to schools that do not allow any digital engagement in the classroom because they know firsthand the all-consuming, addictive nature of what they have created, produced, and promoted. Why are *we* not following suit? The studies are out there. The statistics are undeniable. Why are schools giving in to this? Why do they believe they are offering a better education by offering more technology? Are they bowing to parents' whims? I truly don't understand. Parents need to let the schools run effectively and efficiently so that our children don't fall behind. Technology changes every year. What they are learning about technology now will be obsolete in a very short time. The study skills, research skills, thinking skills, writing skills, reading skills, and even memorization of important facts and figures will benefit them much more.

Teens probably know this more than adults do, though it is our responsibility to monitor and control what flows to our kids. Common sense media claims that 72 percent of teens believe that tech companies manipulate users to spend more time on their devices. Things like rewards for checking in every day, or daily prizes of "gold coins" and the like keep users in a constant state of FOMO (fear of missing out.) Fear, remember, like anger and jealousy is part of our lowest selves, NOT part of our highest and holiest selves.

Critical thinking, consistent values, abiding affections, honor, reverence, moral responsibility, compassion and empathy—any of the qualities that make us more than animals—that make us truly human are all instigated in the prefrontal cortex, the same place where we make good decisions and wise choices. The choices and decisions made with the reptile brain are meant to be used in crisis situations (like being chased by a tiger). Survival, fear, rage, and the energy those primitive emotions create are all important for survival, but they are counterproductive when we are trying to raise thinking, feeling, value-laden, responsible, caring, mature adults.

To date, the pushback against social media has centered around:

- Privacy Concerns: Who has access to our personal information?
- Political Concerns: What is Facebook censoring? What news is Fake News?

But we are not even having the right conversation! Before we can worry about the socio-political aspects of social media, we MUST address the rewiring of the human brain and the "dumbing down" of humanity. Thinking about the entire planet is too big for us though.

It causes us a certain type of paralysis because we know that we can't save everyone. So, let's just concentrate on our circle of influence: children, parents, grandchildren, siblings, extended family, students, church family. Let's begin the conversation there. When your child/teen/nephew/granddaughter/student asks you *why* they must limit their digital engagement, you should be ready to give an answer according to truth—statistical truth, philosophical truth, scientific truth, biblical truth.[19]

What does that look like? How can I do that?

By arming yourself with the basic facts and by constantly using the Word of God as your filter, you can set parameters and boundaries with confidence. Example: **Statistically** there are many predators on social media disguising themselves as kids. 88 percent of teens have seen cyberbullying on social media. The number of sexual assault cases related to social media sites has increased by 300 percent.[20] One in five young people reported having skipped school due to cyberbullying and violence. There is a statistical connection between intensive social media use and mental illness.[21] Everyone should at least have a cursory knowledge of the numbers.

Philosophically I want my children to be fully human, always growing into better versions of themselves, and following the path of sanctification to daily be more Christlike. What does it mean to be fully human? And what does it mean to be Christlike? Of course, you will want to flesh this out for yourself, but here are a few thoughts from philosophers, theologians, and authors to get you started.

On being fully human:

"We must learn to regard people less in the light of what they do or omit to do, and more in the light of what they suffer." --- Deitrich Bonhoeffer

- Balance between the head and the heart
- Realization of and acceptance of our personal fragility and limitations
- Realization of and acceptance of others' limitations and flaws

- Empathy (the ability to understand and share the feelings of another)
- Compassion (concern for the suffering or misfortune of others)
- Emotional connection (the ability to create healthy attachments to other humans)
- The ability to communicate using words, body language, gestures, and facial expressions
- Making our own decisions and bearing the consequences of those decisions
- To think about thinking; to ponder the past, present, and future

On being Christlike:

Because Christ was fully human and fully Divine, we can begin with what it means to be human and add the Divine dimension.

- Loving God with all our heart, mind, body, and soul (Matthew 22:36-40)
- Growing equally in wisdom, stature, and in favor with God and all people (Luke 2:52)
- Being clothed with humility (1 Peter 5:5, Philippians 2:5-8)
- Having affection and grace for others (Romans 12:10)
- Gracious and compassionate, slow to anger, rich in love (Psalm 119:77, Hebrews 4:15)
- Treating others well for healthy relationships (Matthew 22:34-40)
- Communicating the Good News effectively and passionately (Psalm 96:3, Romans 1:16)
- Communicating the Truth with love (Ephesians 4:15)
- Taking personal responsibility for actions and choices (Galatians 6:5, 2 Corinthians 5:10)
- Pondering the past, present, and future from God's perspective (Psalm 90:12)

Scientifically I know that modern tech devices and applications are specifically designed to capture and keep my child's attention (and mine!). I also know that whoever has the most influence in a child's life wins the heart of that child. Influence can be measured in both quantity *and* quality.

How many hours today did my child spend playing video games or looking at her phone? How many hours did my child and I have substantive, value-laden conversation about what is going on in her life? As we age, we become acutely aware that time is limited—it is NOT a renewable resource. Once it has been spent, it can never be retrieved.

I was recently at a church where a baby dedication was taking place. The Children's Ministry team gave each set of parents a jar of marbles. In each jar were 216 marbles. Each marble represents a month of their child's life from birth to the age of 18. The parents were encouraged to remove a marble on the first day of each new month to keep a visual reminder of how little time is left. Any parent who has had teenagers knows that once those teens begin dating, driving, and working they aren't home much. Those last marbles in the jar are slippery and must be held lightly.

Without trying to be morbid, I challenge you to calculate how many months you have left with your precious children. Add that many marbles to a clear jar and keep it in plain sight. Remind yourself that every hour of digital engagement is an hour spent away from your influence, supervision, wisdom, and loving touch. Statistically the average kid will play video games for more than 15 hours per week this summer.[22] If we are talking about time and marbles, then we must calculate this time—NOT by looking at the short range, but at the long range. Fifteen hours a week (and that does not include time on the phone texting, checking social media, watching vapid videos, etc.) means nearly 64 hours a month, more than 760 hours a year. Since there are 730 hours in a month, you just lost a marble to video games every year. Of course, this is not all children, all the time; but it is something to ponder.

Scripturally I know that "As a man thinketh in his heart, so is he." The thoughts our children are thinking while watching YouTube videos, or checking social media, or killing zombies in a video game are not leading to humble, pure, or godly hearts. The substance of what they are watching and participating in is empty (biblical word: "vain"). And I know that time is limited. Most hours spent surfing the net are not hours spent pursuing God or godliness.[23] We are commanded to "redeem the time because the days are evil."[24] There is truly nothing redemptive about most of what we are allowing our kids to be engaged in.

So, this solid square of statistics, philosophical understanding, scientific facts, and scriptural truths become the bedrock or cornerstone of our conversation about digital engagement. It becomes the launching pad for thriving in a digital world.

Do as I say, Not as I Do; Or More is Caught than Taught

It all starts with YOU! Because those in our circles of influence are looking at us adults to lead the way through this quagmire of digital stimulation, they will not fail to notice if we are not "walking the walk." Too many of us "talk the talk" but don't follow through ourselves, and even more of us don't even talk the talk. We've given up with barely a whimper. We wouldn't consider letting our children grow to adults without having talks about the "birds and bees." Most of us have had multiple conversations about drugs and alcohol, peer pressure, bullying, and moral responsibility. Why in the world then would we NOT have the conversations that establish boundaries for digital engagement, including consequences for violating those boundaries? Put it on your calendar this week to have the first of many talks with those who are looking to you for direction and wisdom.

Remember we didn't know what we didn't know, but we do now. Change needs to be made. We need to grab the reins back to safeguard our children and ourselves. The scriptures clearly warn us to look to ourselves first and get our behavior in line with Truth before trying to get anyone else's behavior in line. As we heal ourselves from this prevalent addiction, we will heal our children as well. Then we can truly say without reservation, "Do as I say, AND do as I do!"

Questions to Ponder & Discuss

1. How did you do on the quiz? Do you feel convicted or confident that you have the whole technology usage under control?
2. Who was the first person you thought of that needs to take the quiz?
3. Did you know the "Tech" companies engineer the technology to create addiction? What do you think of that?
4. Did you know that those who create and promote the use of technology do not allow their own children to access it? How does that make you feel?
5. What parameters/boundaries have you set? How effective have they been?
6. Were you surprised how many teens have admitted they have seen cyberbullying on social media?
7. How many months do you have left with your children? It is imperative to realize how many hours a day our children are dedicating to technology.
8. Have you had the conversations with your children, grandchildren, students that establish boundaries for digital engagement? What are the next steps?

THREE

IN DEFENSE OF THE FENCE: THE IMPORTANCE OF BOUNDARIES

"Whatever you are willing to put up with is exactly what you will have."
-Anonymous

When my children were young, we practiced something called, "the interrupt rule" which I learned from Lisa Whetchel's marvelous book, *Creative Correction*. If my children had a question for me while I was talking with someone, instead of the interruption of, "Mom! Mom! Mom…" they were trained to put their hand on my hip. I then acknowledged their need by putting my hand on top of theirs. They had to wait until there was a break in the conversation before I would excuse myself from the adult conversation, turn to my child with the question, and let her have my full attention. Of course, if there were an emergency, I would stop my conversation and immediately see to it. In the present time, I often observe two people having a conversation—an in-depth discussion with eye-to-eye contact, maybe even a boss and an employee. Then ding! A notification comes from one of their phones, and the conversation halts, eye contact is broken, and the continuity of thought is derailed while one impolite person reads what just came across his phone. At any other time in history, this would have been considered unspeakably rude. And guess what? It still is! Why do we do this? And why do we let our children do this?

It Makes Sense to Fence

We can successfully navigate this tech-obsessed world, and help our children achieve this simple and noble goal, but we will need to set good, strong, reasonable boundaries. Let's unpack that for a moment, shall we? A boundary is a line that marks the limit of an area. The purpose of a boundary is to limit something and keep it from something else. Horses in a pasture have the boundary of a fence to keep them from harm. They need a much higher fence than other animals because they are very costly to obtain, and they are very athletic—often jumping over fences. Many equine facilities, ranches, and farms keep "double fences" in case the first fence is jumped by the curious and sometimes headstrong horses.

Our children are of inestimable value—our hearts walking around outside our bodies. They are curious and headstrong as well, so "it makes sense to fence!" Some children in particular are more predisposed to internet addiction. Kids with ADHD, hostility or rage issues, social phobia, or depression can fall into this addiction more easily.[25] *They* won't give you that feedback. *They* will tell you that the parents of every one of their friends place fewer boundaries on technology than you do. *They* will tell you they can handle it (they can't). So, stay strong! Put post-it notes around your home to remind yourself that "It makes sense to fence!"

"Children learn these things from ads: that they are the most important person in the universe, that impulses should not be denied, that pain should not be tolerated, and that the cure for any kind of pain is a product. They learn a weird mix of dissatisfaction and entitlement. With the messages of ads, we are socializing children to be self-centered, impulsive, and addicted. The television teaches values as clearly as any church."[26]

What are Reasonable Boundaries?
Reasonable: *having sound judgment; sensible; prudent.*

No parent ever said, "I hope my child grows up to have poor judgment." As adults we have learned from our own mistakes and from the mistakes of others that poor judgment doesn't make for a happy life. This good judgment that we wish for our children doesn't happen magically when he or she turns 18. There is nothing magical about that number, and just calling them adults at that age doesn't make it so. They learn good judgment, sound judgment by watching *you* make decisions and bear the consequences (more is caught than taught), and by making their own mistakes, then course correcting for success. Much has been said over the years about prudence or sound judgment, including the ideas that the prudent are directly opposite from the foolish, wisdom is found right alongside sound judgment,[27] and those who don't exercise sound judgment (prudence) will suffer for it.[28] Reasonable boundaries, then, are lines that we draw for our children, that are not to be crossed, because we are *prudent* enough to know the harm that lies on the other side of the "fence." And in the end, we want to teach them sound judgment. In fact, some of the more curious and headstrong children may need a "double fence" just to keep them safe!

Some Reasonable Boundaries: Not too soon, and Not too suddenly

I realize that good parenting is the intentional, gradual transfer of power and authority to children as they grow. I am not advocating being "helicopter" parents who hover over their children, but the stakes are too high to allow that transfer of power to happen <u>too soon</u> (before the child has the frontal lobe capability of making good decisions) or <u>too suddenly</u> (just because Grandma bought him a cell phone for his birthday). You will want to flesh these boundaries out for yourself, but many parents tell me they don't even know where to start! Here is a good place to start:

- Time limits for phone usage.
- Not allowing phones during meals.
- Time limits for "free time" on tablets and computers (some homework *must* be done digitally, but make sure they are actually doing homework!)
- Time limits for video games.
- Firm and meaningful (aka "painful") consequences for breaking the technology boundaries ("hopping the fence").
- Phones not allowed in the bedroom during sleep time.

- American Academy of Pediatrics recommends no more than 1-2 hours per day in front of ANY electronics. This includes phones, tablets, computers, video games, and television or movies.[29]
- An hour of outside time for every hour of screen time (younger children).
- An hour of reading for every hour of screen time (older children or times of bad weather).
- No private passwords or unauthorized social media usage.
- No fake accounts that parents don't know about.
- Parents have access to content and history.
- No phone usage (calls/texting) while driving the car.
- Avoid making calls in cars, elevators, trains, and buses. The phone works harder to get signal so the power level of the EMFs increases.
- Limited use of wireless ("Bluetooth") headphones or ear buds because brains and radiation aren't good partners.
- Tell your children not to let anyone, even friends, take pictures or videos of them that could cause embarrassment online or damage their reputation. They should always ask themselves if they would be embarrassed for a relative, teacher, or pastor to see that picture or video.
- Remind kids that even if they delete pictures they have posted, someone has already most likely downloaded it, saved it, or copied it. Don't trust your child's reputation to social media.
- Talk to kids about future consequences since what goes online stays there (somewhere) forever. A 17-year-old might think it funny to post a picture on Facebook of himself looking drunk with empty beer cans around him, but a college admissions office will not find that funny. Potential employers and colleges do check social media.

What are Strong Boundaries?
Strong: *able to withstand great force or pressure.*

As you can imagine, there is going to be a great deal of "pushback" when you start setting boundaries for the first time or start enforcing them for the first time in a long time. Your boundaries must be anchored in truth if they are to withstand the force or pressure of a society that has let their technology usage get out of control and gain the upper hand. Your boundaries must be reasonable, as we mentioned in the last section. And your boundaries must be consistent. We know the truth now, even if we didn't before, that addiction to technology is a real thing and it's a dangerous thing. We know the truth now that spending hours a day reacting quickly and violently to "threats" in a video game predisposes teens to angry, retaliatory, knee-jerk responses to any and all perceived threats.[30] We know now that the radiation coming off a typical smartphone is extremely detrimental to the developing brains of children. The bones of a child's skull are different than those of an adult. A child's skull is only a fraction of the strength of an adult skull, and the gaps (bone sutures) between the skull bones are weaker as well.[31] The bones of the skull do not completely fuse together until the age of twenty.[32] This allows for much higher absorption of harmful radiation from the electric and magnetic fields (EMFs) that accompany electronics. Many countries around the world ban wireless technology in preschools for this very reason. Wireless tablets, headphones, game controllers, and laptop computers all emit strong radiation that causes brain disruption and cellular damage.

What are Good Boundaries?
Good: *morally excellent, virtuous.*

"Finally, brothers and sisters, whatever is true, whatever is noble, whatever is right, whatever is pure, whatever is lovely, whatever is admirable—if anything is excellent or praiseworthy—think about such things."[33]

The word "Christian" indicates one who is a disciple (student) or follower of Jesus. Anyone who wants to be successful in his faith life and leave a lasting legacy of faith for generations to follow uses Christ as his example. This same Jesus is found in the Bible from the book of Genesis to the book of Revelation. He is patterned and promised throughout writings that predate his birth by thousands of years, but it's not just the pattern and promise of Messiah that we see in the Old Testament, it is Christ himself![34] What does His word have to say about the subjects of time, boundaries, and the foundations, fruits, and motivations of the digital world?

On Time:

As humans, we have only three resources: time, energy, and money, and we are called to be good managers or stewards of each of them. We are called to walk in wisdom, making the most of our time.[35] We are told that we should do good works now while we can since the night is coming when no one can work.[36] In the last year especially I can see that the "night" is coming. The world is distorted, distressed, diseased, discouraged, and downtrodden. I wonder how many church members are "asleep" in their souls, wasting time daily with a dopamine addiction, not doing the good works that are desperately needed in the world—works that are necessary to make faith alive.[37] We are told that the hour has come for us to wake up from sleep—to rouse ourselves to love and good works.[38] We are told to look carefully at how we are living our lives, being careful to walk not as unwise, but as wise—making the best use of our time because the days we live in are evil.[39] We are told that if "we snooze, we lose!"[40] We are told that there is a time for everything, and everything has a time boundary.[41] And we are warned that we shouldn't boast ourselves that there will be a tomorrow, because we don't know what a day may bring.[42]

If today were our last one on earth, would we spend it staring at a screen? Neither should our children.

> *"And morality refers not only to sex and violence*
> *but also to the use of power, time,*
> *and money. Broadly defined, morality is about*
> *making decent and wise choices*
> *about how to be in the universe. It implies*
> *purposeful action for the common good."*[43]

On Boundaries

The word *boundaries* is popular in the world of psychology and counseling. The Bible doesn't specifically use this word (especially in the older translations), but it still has a lot to say about boundaries. The writer of Proverbs 25 tells us to not wear out our welcome by spending too much time in our neighbor's house. Wouldn't that apply to constant texting and digital communication as well? Just a thought. God has determined the allotted periods and the boundaries of all mankind.[44] The Psalmist recognizes that God has laid out the lines and boundaries of his life.[45] Time itself is a boundary. In the beginning, God set the boundary of a 24-hour day, with the sun to rule by day and the moon and stars to rule by night.[46] The wild waves of the sea even have a boundary. God says, "You can come this far, but no farther!"[47] When He marked out the foundations of the earth (another boundary), He set a boundary for the sea so that the water would not transgress His command.[48] Everything in God's creation has boundaries. These boundaries are reasonable (they have a reason), they are strong (they hold up under pressure), and they are good (they are morally without reproach). Why in the world wouldn't we follow this pattern and keep these kinds of boundaries in our home? One word: *pressure*.

On the Foundations and Fruits of Digital Entertainment

I will reiterate here that I am not a Luddite. Technology is here to stay, and I'm okay with that! But as with the emergence of any new technology, there must be rules! When fire was discovered, there had to be rules to keep people from being burned or burning others. When the nuclear bomb was invented, there had to be global rules governing the use of that kind of deadly technology. Any national leader who flouts these rules is considered by the rest of the world to be dangerous and/or deranged. So, must there be rules governing our families' use of technology. The stakes are too high, the consequences too grave, the time too short to do otherwise.

We don't fully know what the outcome of an entire generation raised with constant use of digital technology will look like. We are in a grand, social experiment that won't be able to be undone once it has been accomplished. The best analogy for this generational experiment is cigarette smoking. Years ago, no one knew the health implications of smoking, though many have argued that the cigarette manufacturers were fully aware. Doctors smoked and even recommended certain types of cigarettes.[49] Consumers were told that "doctors recommend" certain brands with menthol to help with the smoker's cough. Because we didn't know the dangers, we never considered setting boundaries on tobacco products. Nor did we consider educating families on those dangers. We didn't know what we didn't know. But now we know!

Here's what we know *now* about digital engagement:

- Kids are losing focus in the classroom. Learning is hard work and doesn't give the *dopamine ding*. Teachers can't compete with the stimulation afforded by digital engagement.
- Kids are on tablets, phones, computers, and other devices all day, every day, even at school.
- A study conducted back in 2014 indicated that 8-18-year-olds spend an average of 7.5 hours per day on social media alone! How is this possible when they are in school most of the day? Yes, you got it! They are distracted with it at school.
- Kids are not being educated fully if they are distracted. If your child has texted you or responded to your text during the school day, then they are texting and responding to other people as well.
- Loneliness, depression anxiety[50], bullying, lack of focus, pornography exposure and potential addiction,[51]comparison, envy, exhaustion, and suicide[52] are all being linked to the misuse and overuse of technology.[53]

"The world is changing, and we need to change with it," you may say. But ask yourself this: "At what price does that change come?" With all the changes in how we relate; or don't relate to others, is it possible that we are changing our very identity as humans? Some experts believe so. A recent article in The Daily Mail explores the idea that because of technology, we as humans are having an "identity crisis" that goes right to the heart of humanity, affecting how we view ourselves, interact with others, decide what makes us happy, and ultimately determines our ability to reach our full potential as human beings. The author is a researcher at Oxford University who has seen the "rewiring" of the human brain not figuratively, but literally at a microcellular level with the constant use of technology. He states that today's technology is creating a marked shift in the way we *think,* the way we *act,* and the way we *feel.*

One area we are changing is in the "give and take" that is thick and vibrant in a true community but lacking in the global, digital community. In real life, when we want something from another, we ask politely, not sure if it will be given to us. We offer up a barter, a bargain, or just go belly up and admit our ignorance—but there is no demanding past the age of toddlerhood. In the digital community we demand, we seek, we get; but we don't give back. We want to know—What is the fastest route home? Why do I have pain in my abdomen? How do I bake a loaf of bread or thread a needle? We demand and we get instantaneously. That is not a recipe for a fully developed human being. It breeds a selfishness and narcissism that can currently be seen everywhere.

There is also the matter of accountability—another area in which humans are changing because of overuse and abuse. There is an old Latin phrase, *Esse Quam Videri,* which means "To be rather than to seem to be." This was first written by Cicero in his essay *On Friendship.* His point was that *many* want to be seen as having virtue; but *few* want to actually be virtuous. Today this is known as "virtue signaling." Roman virtues were character qualities such as dignity, hospitality, self-control, humor, tenacity, frugality, etc.—qualities that we could all agree are good for humans to possess. These are not qualities that are valued or encouraged in the world of digital engagement. Remember, that is our primary goal—to create fully developed human beings!

The foundations of digital entertainment (social media, games, videos, memes, vines, pics, stories, pins, snapchats, tweets, etc.) are not neutral. Remember back to the section about the race for the bottom of the brain stem and you will now connect the dots that the very foundations of this entertainment is a competition for who will control the minds and wills of humans. The creators of this entertainment acknowledge this, so why are *we* reluctant to acknowledge it? Entertainment itself is a-musement. Muse means to think. Entertainment is non-thinking, which is great once and a while. But how many total hours a day are we spending NOT thinking? Look at your screen time usage, and you will be surprised. Log the hours of screen time your children have, and you will be shocked by that as well. Remember to count the time at school in front of screens, Sunday School, children's church, homework, and at the houses of their friends. If the foundation of something is flawed, then so is the rest of that something.[54] If our children are allowed to build their lives (time is life), on the foundation of amusement, when the flood of adult responsibilities, and the tests of character and trials of faith come along—when the flood waters rise and beat vehemently on their lives—they will not stand.[55]

The fruits of digital entertainment are far different than the fruits of the Spirit. The more time we spend under the guidance and sanctifying grace of the Holy Spirit, the more love, joy, peace, patience, kindness, gentleness, goodness, faithfulness, and self-control we will have.[56] After spending an entire evening playing video games, does your child exhibit more or fewer of these characteristics? How about the fruit of the sinful nature that we all carry—idolatry. Let's just park here for a minute.

I've heard it said that we can measure the strength of an idol in our lives by how upset we are if it is taken from us. How do your children react when told they can't play video games, or use their phone at the table? My guess is, not well. The other fruits of the flesh like impurity, sensuality, lack of self-control, hostility, strife, jealousy, fits of anger, disputes, envy, and riotous behavior are often amplified by excessive digital engagement. The fruit of a tree determines what kind of tree it is, so the fruit of our children's lives tells others what they are all about.

On the Motivations of Social Media and Digital Entertainment

Ultimately, the goal of social media platforms, video games, and most all digital engagement is to make money off the consumer. Their motivation is no less suspect than the Madison Avenue executives who dressed actors up in white coats to look like doctors and then had them promote cigarettes as a healthful way to deal with stress. Nothing could be further from the truth. We know this now because even after more than 20 years of education and limiting advertising of tobacco products, and raising the legal age of smoking, still more than 154,000 people will die this year in our nation from lung cancer.

In 20 years, given the current overuse and misuse of technology, we may very well be seeing "adults" who don't know how to engage in a real conversation; who don't know how to read a real book; who don't know how to put off their need for instant gratification and constant a-musement. Imagine your grandchildren and their children unable to sustain normal friendships and love relationships because they have not spent the time and energy developing these virtues. This is a tragedy we can't afford to sit back and watch. We must engage by conversation, education, and strong, true, reasonable, and good boundaries. It makes sense to fence.

Questions to Ponder & Discuss

1. Do you think it is rude while you are talking with someone, they look at their phone to read a text, respond to a ding?
2. Have you ever said that to someone? What was their reaction?
3. What are reasonable boundaries? Give examples.
4. Have you set time limits for phone usage? For yourself? Your family?
5. Where are phones during meals?
6. What consequences have you set if boundaries are broken?
7. Do you check your children's phone? Why or why not?
8. Do you monitor your screen time usage? What about your children's?
9. How do your children react when they are told they can't play video game or use their phone/tablet?

FOUR

TOOLS OF THE TRADE: MINDSETS

"I suppose it is tempting, if the only tool you have is a hammer,
to treat everything as if it were a nail."
-Abraham Maslow—Law of the Instrument

After reading the first three chapters of this book, you may be having one of two different, opposite reactions. You may be thinking, "This is just basic parenting, and I can use the tools I already have in my toolbox to handle the overuse and misuse of technology by my family members." Or, you may be thinking, "Yikes! This problem is overwhelming! I don't even know where to start regulating this *digital toxin* that has wormed its way into my family." I would challenge you that there is a third way.

This digital onslaught took all of us by surprise with its speed, strength, scope, and sway. The tools we acquired years ago are not necessarily going to work by themselves. The thought of tackling this "monster" can be overwhelming, but it doesn't have to be! The Spirit that resides in us brings power—in the Greek, *Dunamahee* which means "to make possible." The power of the Spirit is the power of *I can!* All that remains is your willingness to use the tools available to take in hand the reins of your family life. YOU should be controlling the plans, purposes, and passions of your family! Don't give up that power and authority (one synonym of *power* is *influence*) that God has given to you as parents, grandparents, teachers, and the like. Don't give it up to a bunch of social scientists who are racing to the bottom of your child's brain stem. Leverage that influence to keep the trajectory of your children's lives on course for success. So, how exactly do we do that?

I'm so glad you asked. First let's cover the mindsets that you must have to be successful in this venture. Then we will make available some methods that are out there for ensuring your success.

Speed, Strength, Scope, and Sway

If we are going to wage a successful campaign, we must first know the face of our "enemy." In the classic work, *The Art of War,* the author Sun Tzu reminds us that, "If you know the enemy and know yourself, you need not fear the result of a hundred battles. If you know yourself but not the enemy, for every victory gained you will also suffer a defeat. If you know neither the enemy nor yourself, you will succumb in every battle." In this case, the "enemy" is the misuse, overuse, and abuse of technology by our children. We need to understand what it is capable of and what it isn't capable of. We need to know its strengths and its weaknesses. Then we need to find a way to mitigate its strengths and take advantage of its weaknesses. That is the essence of a successful campaign.

Speed

If you want a glimpse of how things have sped up, get your family together and watch an old movie. No, not that old…. I'm not talking about black and white, or about silent films. I'm talking about watching a movie from the late 1970s to the late 1980s—just a mere 40 years ago. You may not notice the slowness of the pace, or the long stretches not filled with background music, or the underwhelming saturation of color, but your children will notice! They will easily get bored and probably ask to watch something else. Even if they enjoy a classic like, *Back to the Future,* or *Groundhog Day,* they won't be overwhelmed by it. They may think it's cute or mildly funny, but they won't be "blown away." When asked, young adults from Millennials to Generation Alpha to Gen Z to iGen offer similar opinions:

- "It just feels lazy."
- "It's so slow it's boring."

- "The cinematography is underwhelming."
- "It's subpar in quality."

Is it subpar in quality? Or have our tastes changed? I believe you know the answer to that. The good part about the blazing speed of today's digital engagement *should be* productivity, but when I look around, I truly don't see that people in general are more productive than they used to be. They are busier, but not necessarily more productive. Some are, to be sure, but most aren't. Most are "multi-tasking", which is a fancy word for being distracted and not being wholehearted. If a roomful of employers were canvassed, I doubt the majority of them would say that their employees are much more productive than they were twenty years ago. What we CAN be sure of is that the appetite for rapidly shifting images, overwhelmingly rich graphics, color saturation and vibrancy, and the need for instant gratification that this speed conditions one to is at an all-time high. These sub-generations can't remember the world before the internet. They grew up swiping an iPad before they learned how to talk and are the first generation to be raised in the era of smartphones. Teenage members of Gen Z are connected nearly every waking hour of the day.[57] This digital saturation creates a certain "taste" by arranging neural patterns in the brain to expect more of the same. Because slower, real life experiences cannot measure up, kids can get hopeless, bored, and cynical. Remember when our moms taught us not to eat sweets before dinner because it would "ruin our appetite?" Yeah. We need those voices now.

What's So Dangerous About Speed?

There is no way that regular, everyday life can compete with this type of ramped up, constant entertainment. School life surely can't. Teachers struggle. A friend who is a 3rd grade teacher told me a story of what recently happened in her classroom. She has taught for years and has always paired students up to work together. This year was the first year she had many students not wanting to work in pairs but rather asking to work alone. She did not give them the option to work alone because there is great value in learning to cooperate as part of a team to reach a final outcome. She has noticed kids today live in their own bubbles, not wanting to engage with other students, no eye contact or communication. This is a problem because in real life they will need to be able to communicate and work with others. Another friend is a kindergarten teacher, and she observes that students are entering kindergarten not knowing how to cut and color— lacking basic tactical skills. They know how to "swipe," but not how to even hold a pencil or scissors. This initial lack of prerequisite, tactile skills is very harmful to a student's academic development.

Kids are losing focus in the classroom. If your child came home and told you that their school had turned on televisions, had music blaring and lights flickering, you would immediately call the school insisting that the distractions cease. Everyone knows that is not an ideal learning environment, however kids are on their devices all day long, admitting they are losing focus in the classroom. While the average US adult spends 38 minutes per day on Facebook, 16 to 24-year-olds spend a median of three hours a day on social media alone[58] and several more hours viewing YouTube videos. YouTube has 30 million active users daily. People watch 5 billion videos a day on YouTube. And the average viewing session on YouTube is 40 minutes. 81 percent of all parents with children age 11 or younger let them watch videos on YouTube with 34 percent saying that they allow them to do this on a regular basis. In addition, this same survey shows that 61 percent of these same parents say their children have encountered content on YouTube that was unsuitable for a child to watch.[59]

When do they have time to do all this? Obviously, they are doing some of it at school! While in the classroom they are not paying attention because they are on their devices. If your child has texted you or responded to you while in class during the school day, I am sure you are not the only one they are texting. That might be their intent, but it is all too tempting (actually addicting) to look at their phones. Why are we allowing this to affect our children's scholastic development? The ramped-up stimulation of so much digital engagement affects the neural pathways of the brain, making old-fashioned learning more difficult and sleep hard to come by. Rudimentary education is key to long term success, and sleep plays a huge role in our ability to function every day for several reasons:

- It is only during sleep that stress hormones are metabolized.
- Poor sleep quality is associated with maladaptive changes in the stress pathways of the body.[60]
- The changes in the body from a heightened stress response markedly increase the potential for metabolic disorders like obesity and diabetes.
- Heightened stress response diminishes immune function and causes brain shrinkage.

Only bad things happen quickly. All the good stuff takes time. Think about the things that have changed your life in a moment—they are nearly all bad: car accidents, calls in the middle of the night, a doctor's pronouncement of cancer. Other than a last-minute score that wins a ball game, little else good happens suddenly.[61] Learning new things, changing old behaviors, building character and satisfying relationships, saving money, raising children, and leaving a lasting legacy—these things all take time.[62]

Slow Your Roll

God ordained the family at creation, and desired both then and now that they be healthy, whole, connected, and reflective of His glory. Because the hectic pace of modern, digitally-enhanced life causes both parents and children to feel empty, depleted, and disconnected, it's important to have some basic strategies for slowing down family life and then practicing those strategies until they become part of the fabric of your routine. These slow threads will make the tapestry you are creating much more interesting, enjoyable, and long-lasting. Legacies don't happen quickly. They happen slowly—thread by thread. Child development consists of more than pouring information into a child. Rather it is a process of unfolding for the child—unfurling like a flower into his best and most beautiful self.[63] This nurturing on the part of parents and unfolding on the part of children takes quality time and quantity of time. There are no shortcuts. The biggest argument for slowing down the pace of the family is integration. Just as sleep integrates experiences and makes memories out of sensory experiences, pausing regularly for long enough integrates information with personality and character. This is true for both adults and children, but because children's brains are still formative, it is crucial to have regular "down time" so that they can integrate the information that they are bombarded with all day every day. Today's parent peer pressure is to speed up, sign up, join up, and hurry up. Slow family living as defined by one author is simple: slow down, connect, and enjoy each other.[64]

> *When kids have time to integrate, they stay*
> *emotionally and physiologically resourced.*
> *When they are resourced, they are more present,*
> *more compassionate, and more connected.*[65]

Strength & Sway

Strength refers to the ability to withstand pressure or force. The strength of digital engagement lies in the fact that barring an electro-magnetic pulse from a foreign enemy that shuts down life as we know it, technological saturation is here to stay. We can't wish it away. We must have a plan. *Sway* refers to a level of subjugation or control. We talked earlier in this book about the strong, addictive nature of digital engagement. One area we didn't get into was internet pornography, which is highly addictive— some say more addictive than heroin, cocaine, and nicotine.[66] Erectile dysfunction is rampant among 18-25 year old young men who have no physical reason for this condition. The common denominator in this group is regular digital consumption of pornography.[67] We won't go into this important topic here because it constitutes an entire book on its own, since 30 percent of all data transferred across the internet is porn.[68] I only mention it here to emphasize the strength and sway of digital engagement with our children. In the resources, I will share some helpful websites and books related to this topic.

The strength of this pull on the minds and affections of our families can't be overstated. Neither can the sway of the social (peer) pressure to keep up with all of it. Whether it's the pre-teen boy whose peers all play video games online for hours a day instead of meeting up in real life, or the young teen girl who gets shamed for not having the latest, greatest phone, or the high school student who commits suicide as a result of cyberbullying.

The strength and sway of this entire dynamic are overwhelming! How can a parent fight it? Most don't. Most give in and throw up their hands. After all, who wants their child to be "the weird one" who isn't allowed to follow the others off the cliff like so many lemmings?

There exists a natural and normal hierarchy of trust and affection in the heart and mind of a child. Children naturally trust their primary caregivers unless those caregivers prove themselves unworthy of trust. Even then, it is difficult to sway the affections of a child away from his parents. We have seen this hierarchy in play for thousands of years. Anytime it has been upset or altered, it has not been beneficial. I won't go down through history with a list of examples. Here we will focus on one prime, but not isolated example.

Young people were crucial to the agenda of the Nazis under Adolf Hitler. He set about to influence children both inside and outside of school by means of indoctrination—all under the guise of state-run education. All teachers had to join the Nazi Teachers' Association (Union) and they had to attend training in the summers to make sure their teaching was solidly in line with the Nazi Party. This teacher's union decided if those teachers were politically suitable to train Germany's youth. The textbooks were rewritten with the government's agenda taking precedence over facts and truth. The curriculum in schools was altered to reflect government priorities and agendas. Religious education was banned one step at a time.[69] The Hitler Youth took over all youth movements in Germany, except Catholic youth groups. These were eventually eliminated as well. The quality and scope of education deteriorated under this system. Children were given more freedom from their parents, and national slogans encouraged the Youth to lead the nation. The Nazis were experts at engineering history to serve their party's political purposes by alienating the natural affections of children from their parents.

Does any of this sound familiar to you? It should. For several generations, there has been a concerted effort underway to rid public schools of religions of faith, replacing them with the religion of first humanism, then pluralism, then multiculturalism, and now Marxism. Children like Greta Thunberg[70] have been shoved into the spotlight, forcing older generations to bow to the "wisdom" of children and the cult of youth, ignoring the truth that, "foolishness is bound up in the heart of a child, but the rod of correction drives it far from him." The rod of correction has nothing to do with corporal punishment (spanking). When a shepherd took care of his sheep, he had a rod that he used to pull sheep back from danger and lead them into green pastures and beside still waters. It takes a parent's regular prodding, direction, and re-direction to help children become wise.[71]

As parents we are sometimes too close to the woods to see the trees. We don't always realize that the time, money, and energy spent on digital tools (mostly tools of entertainment, not learning) is a strong influence that upsets the natural affections and hierarchy of parents and children. If you have ever begged, cajoled, scolded, threatened, or bribed your child to stop playing video games or put away her phone during a meal, then the balance has already been upset. It's time to restore that balance for the sake of your family.

Scope

Scope refers to the extent or reach of a thing. In this case, we are talking about the scope of digital use, overuse, and abuse. The statistics I have shared all through these chapters are enough to show the scope of control that digital platforms have in our families. All these statistics were published before this most recent pandemic crisis that has driven most students to online learning (constant digital engagement). More statistics will not persuade you more—it will only serve to make you more discouraged. After all, we can't save the whole world! Or the whole country. Or the whole neighborhood. But we are called to be accountable for what goes on inside the walls of our homes. We are called to be accountable for our stewardship of:

- Time (quantity & quality)
- Treasure (money & strength)
- Talents (gifts & abilities)
- Touch (influence & inspiration)
- Testimony (truth & values)

Most of us have seen families in restaurants—each member looking down at a phone. No one is talking. They aren't present or connected to each other; instead they are connected to whatever is capturing their attention at the moment. Somewhere deep inside we know that this is upsetting the natural balance and affection of families, but we forget. We need to be reminded, and we need to remind those we care about. One reason is that we will statistically spend many more years with our children as adults than we do with them as children. Beginning with the end in mind, we want to focus not on raising good children but on raising productive adults.

Slowing down the family results in a more connected and joyful family life now and down the road 20, 30, and 40 years from now. We want our children to participate in the wonderful world of capitalism and personal achievement, but what we don't need or want is for our children to be trapped in *Surveillance Capitalism*—an economic system centered around the commodification of personal data with the core purpose of profit-making. We want all our family members to be truly connected in real life to others, not just digitally to images and profiles. We want our future adult children to have rich, godly, and satisfying sexual connection with a spouse of their choosing. What they don't need is to go into relationships saddled with addictions and rewired brains from oversexualization at an early age. We want our kids to be entranced by the beauty and wonder of nature, not under the spell of false worlds that don't exist except to capitalize financially from the participants. What we want is for our children to grow to be rich, real, fully functional humans who can communicate clearly, love passionately, work diligently, and at the end of the day, be content with their life choices. This doesn't happen without a lot of intentional work.

Questions to Ponder & Discuss

1. How is technology the "enemy" in your household?
2. Does multi-tasking make you more productive? Why or why not?
3. When are you NOT connected to your phone? How does that make you feel?
4. What can you do to build "down time" into your child's day?
5. How often do you connect as a family without any digital devices?
6. Have you noticed a difference in your child's behavior:
   a. After watching YouTube videos? b. After gaming? c. After school?
7. Are you and/or your children more peaceful after you have been disconnected from your devices for a period of time?
8. Have you noticed a shift in your personal relationships i.e., friends, family, co-workers?
   More or less connected?
9. What steps can you take to restore the balance within your family?

FIVE

TOOLS OF THE TRADE: METHODS

What Can You Do Now?

If you are a parent, then these suggestions are for you. If you are a grandparent, then you can exercise your considerable influence to offer these suggestions in the spirit, not of judgment, but of love and care. If you are a teacher, coach, or minister, you can gear your teaching around these principles—reminding children, parents, and families about what is important, and what is not. There are some easy fixes like a digital curfew where at a certain time of night all electronics are turned off until the "curfew" is over the next day. Or buying an old-fashioned alarm clock to get you up in the mornings instead of having the temptation and distraction of a cell phone looking at you the minute you awaken. There are contracts that can be made, and parental controls that can be put into place. You must wade through these options and decide which ones work best for your family. Particularly challenging is the situation where you have children in different stages of life. Obviously, the rules will be different for an elementary student than for a high school student. To do nothing however, is not an option if you want to recapture the heart of your family.

Most importantly know you are not alone. Do not give up! It takes time to break the addiction to technology. Don't look at the elephant in the room but look at the little chunks you can change. As the old saying goes, "The way to eat an elephant is one bite at a time." Over time you can make a difference if you set a course and stay the course. Find a balance that is right for you and your family.

1. Meals are sacred

Change is hard. Nobody likes to be changed except a wet baby—and even then, they cry. Once you establish the rule of "no phones at the table," then it will be common understanding. Getting past the initial "blowback" from kids who have been used to freewheeling with their phones anytime and anyplace will be a challenge. Although your God-given parental authority (the power to carry out responsibility) should be enough to help you carry this out, parents today are much more "democratic" with their children than parents of previous generations. Whether this is beneficial or not is not for me to say, but it does make exerting authority more difficult if you haven't done much of it in the past—or if you haven't stuck with decisions long-term. Kids need consistency more than anything, so if you make this rule, be ready to stick to it no matter what. If it helps, you can use the following information to help sway the decision.

Back in the day, families said "grace" before eating—a nod to God's constant provision and half a minute of shown gratitude. Believe it or not, there are scientific findings that support this practice as a way to enhance health and well-being. It's called "mindful eating." If you've ever scarfed down a meal while driving, you probably didn't enjoy more than the first bite, and likely you don't remember the meal at all. You didn't savor the food or the experience. New research shows that any type of small ritual like a short prayer of thankfulness or cooking together enhances the experience, and makes us eat more slowly, savoring the food. People who are thankful for their food are better able to cope with stress, have more positive emotions, and are better able to reach their goals. Visionary researcher Dr. Masaru Emoto shows through numerous experiments that positive human thoughts and emotions like gratitude (e-motions = energy in motion) can alter the molecular structure of our bodies and the foods we put into them.[72] So taking a moment to put away the phones and offer thanks seems a reasonable and simple change that will make a big difference. While you are at it, why not keep those phones put down and establish some other rituals. One of my favorites is to go around the table while eating and ask each person, "What was the best part of your day?" "What was the worst part of your day?" In this way you will establish a safe place for emotional transparency and another ritual. Rituals themselves are "touchstones of remembrance" meaning that your children may not remember the chicken, but they will remember the conversations. Another benefit of this ritual is that you truly get to know what your kids are going through and what they have taken away from their daily experiences. This information is gold. Use it later (not at the table) to teach, mentor, advise, exhort, or challenge. They are giving you the keys to the kingdom of their hearts.

2. The art of asking people to put away their phones

I ask myself why we are so scared to tell a friend to put their phone down and spend time with us. I am here now; I may not be later. We need to have the courage to speak truth in love. After many years of frustration and sadness with all I have seen with the onslaught of technology, what finally prompted me to write this book is when a friend and I were trying to navigate the landscape of going out to dinner without being on our devices. She had a senior in high school who would be driving that night, so she wanted to make sure he was safe. I understood that. I had two teenaged girls at the time. I recommended that she turn the ringer on and put her phone on "do not disturb." Those in her favorites would ring through even though her phone was in "do not disturb" mode. She would then need to be intentional and tell her children if they needed her in an emergency to call her. I think our emergencies are different today. We tell ourselves the story that we need to respond to everything immediately which affects our conversations, mealtimes, dates, work environments, no matter what the situation—our overall togetherness is disrupted. It's a simple thing to turn on this common phone feature to protect the time you are spending with others. One of the most basic needs we as humans have is to be truly heard and seen. The *do not disturb* feature makes this possible.

Married couples allow phones into their bedrooms effectively bringing in a third person as each person talks, texts, or messages that third person. We would be appalled at someone actually being in our shared bed, but isn't that what is happening when you are answering texts while sitting next to the person that at one time you couldn't wait to marry? Why has this happened? We had no idea the damage that would result in loneliness, depression, anxiety, and the break-up of marriages. We need to make changes to reestablish boundaries and preserve what is truly important.

That meme on Instagram isn't important. Time with your mate is. You can thrive amid this ever changing, ever evolving tech-obsessed landscape *if you choose to.*

Some ways to get the other to engage and be present:

- You seem really busy. Should we shoot for another time together instead of now?
- Would you mind waiting until we are done to use your phone?
- It would be great to have your attention; I know many others want it right now too. What are your thoughts?
- Hey, can you please put your phone away?
- I understand your desire to multitask, but I'm all about being fully present and emotionally engaged.

3. Digital curfew

Curfews are put into place to protect those under the curfew. Just as you wouldn't want your teenager roaming the streets of your city in the middle of the night, you shouldn't want him or her roaming the avenues of the internet either. It's likely far more dangerous! Make kids turn off and hand to you their tablets, phones, etc. at least one hour before bedtime. This does several things. It forces them to get quiet in their minds, focusing on a good book or their own thoughts. It also stops the influx of "blue light" that radiates from all electronic screens.

Americans spend an average of 7 hours a day on electronic devices, bathing their eyes and brains with light in the 400-490 nanometer range—which is "blue light." Blue light revs up the side of the brain that is the "gas," while suppressing the side that is the "brakes." At night we need to put on the brakes from the day, not keep pushing the gas pedal. Exposure to all colors of light affects your natural Circadian rhythm (sleep/wake cycle), and in the visible light spectrum, blue light has the most power to affect your body clock.

Our eyes aren't good at blocking blue light, so it passes relatively unfiltered to the brain. More than any other color, blue light interferes with the body's ability to process melatonin—the hormone that makes us feel sleepy. I've known some parents who don't require this, but then they have their kids pop a melatonin supplement to feel sleepy. This is not the best way to approach sleep issues. Exposure to television, smartphones, tablets, gaming systems, fluorescent light bulbs, LED bulbs, and computer monitors at night almost guarantee sleep that is less than optimally restful.[73] Set an alarm an hour before you want to be in bed to remind you to turn off all electronics. This is a simple fix, but it requires self-discipline.

4. Balancing the brain

Screen time tends to give kids "tunnel vision" which is detrimental to their overall learning and development. Tunnel vision is stressed-based perception, and it focuses on one or two narrow objects while the entire world around the viewer is going on at full tilt! Nearly half of all children ages eight and younger own their own tablet devices and spend at least 2-3 hours per day on them according to Common Sense Media. A landmark study from the National Institutes of Health in 2018 showed that kids who spend more than two hours per day on screen type activities (even educational ones) showed thinning of the cortex in the brain—the area related to reasoning and critical thinking. Tunnel vision is for survival—it wasn't meant to be a constant way of life in humans.[74] Tunnel vision gives rise to impulsivity—the exact opposite of the skills needed for long term success.

Staying hypervigilant or what's known as a heightened sympathetic state for long periods of time, or for shorter periods of time, but on a regular basis limits our capacity to make good decisions. This isn't moralizing; it's the science of neurobiology. Teach your child to balance his brain with as much outdoor activity as indoor. So, for every hour of game time or screen time, the child must log an hour gardening, biking, playing with friends, exercising outdoors, fishing, swimming, skating, watching the clouds, building a tree house, or simply sitting in the grass reading a book. Balance is key to all things.

5. 30-day digital detox/mind reset

This would be a really cool thing for families to do all together. It's definitely a "team builder" when all members of the family are struggling with the same challenge. The author of a fabulous article in Forbes magazine[75] created the 30-day digital detox challenge after a friend begged her to create something to help keep technology from taking over the friend's life. This article is an abbreviated version of the program outlined in her book, *The Power of Off: The Mindful Way to Stay Sane in a Virtual World.* Here are some highlights:

6 Simple Things to Do Before You Start

1. Create a log. Choose one workday or a full workweek, as well as one weekend, to track your use of all tech devices. Determine the No. 1 behavior you want to cut down on or eliminate, which may involve multiple devices.
2. Find a partner. Sharing your experience with another person will help make you accountable for your behavior and for sticking with the detox.
3. Contemplate. Identify five negative consequences of your technology use and five positive results that will come from cutting down or changing your technology use.

    Support yourself. Write and post statements such as "I want to be in control of my choices around technology" around your home, car, and office.

    Move your computer to a less comfortable place in your home.

    Buy a new journal for this detox. At the end of each day, write down something (length is unimportant) about your experience with the process.

Doing the 30-Day Tech Detox

The 30-Day Tech Detox is cumulative — with each new prescription, you will continue to practice the previously prescribed actions. So, for example, on Day 5, you will be practicing five new behaviors, the behavior of Day 5 and those from Days 1, 2, 3 and 4. By Day 30, you will be practicing 30 new behaviors. If a prescription doesn't apply to that particular day (for example, "Refrain from use during exercising"), switch it with a day when it does. Now, the important part: action!

Day 1. Pay attention to and internally note every time you feel the impulse or hear the thought to check one of your devices or computers. When you notice this, ask yourself, "Am I checking out of habit?" and "Is this checking necessary right now?" If the answer is "Habit" or "Not Necessary," then repeat to yourself "Stop" and do just that. Simultaneously, designate three times in the day when you are allowed to check your device, whether necessary or not.

Day 2. Refrain from any tech use when socializing or otherwise interacting with people. This includes everyone — shopkeepers, waiters, and service people as well as your family and friends.

Day 3. Refrain from holding your device in your hand or keeping it in your pocket when it's not in use. Store it out of sight elsewhere.

Day 4. Refrain from using any of your devices during the first hour after you wake up in the morning. If your smartphone is also your alarm clock, treat it as such. Turn it completely off as soon as it's sounded your morning wake-up.

Day 5. Refrain from using tech devices during the last hour before you go to bed.

Day 6. Turn off all alerts and notifications on your device. If your cell phone is your alarm clock, leave only the alarm notification intact.

Day 7. Refrain from using your devices on public transportation or in taxis.

Day 8. Write down four activities or experiences that nourish your spirit. Keep these simple and accessible — not the climbing-to-the-summit-of-Mount-Everest sort. Give yourself one of these experiences today and get one on the calendar for each week to come. This practice should continue weekly after your detox as well.

Day 9. Refrain from using your devices while waiting in line — any kind of line.

Day 10. Refrain from using technology in the car, except when you need GPS assistance.

Day 11. Refrain from using while waiting for something to begin, such as a movie, a play, a concert, or a social interaction.

Day 12. Refrain from using during events — for example, at concerts, the theater, or children's recitals.

Day 13. Make your bathroom a tech-free zone.

Day 14. Refrain from using technology while walking on the street.

Day 15. Make your bedroom a tech-free zone. Remove all devices and computers and refrain from using in the room or area where you sleep.

Day 16. Set aside two continuous three-hour blocks of time in the day when you will be tech-free. This can be scheduled on a weekend day if it is impossible during the workweek.

Day 17. Refrain from using while exercising unless you are providing yourself with music.

Day 18. Refrain from immediately using the internet to research non-work-related information that you have forgotten or want to know — for example, looking up the name of a television actor or the year a song was released. Wait at least 24 hours before going online to find out the answer, if the answer hasn't already occurred to you.

Day 19. If there is a website that is particularly addictive for you, sign up for Net Nanny or another service that prevents you from accessing it.

Day 20. Refrain from tech use while cooking and eating.

Day 21. Refrain from using when walking or being in nature.

Day 22. Commit to one tech-free day per month — the third Sunday of the month, for example. Now, enter these dates into your calendar for the rest of the year — and stick to them. Tell those close to you that you will not be available via your devices on that day of the month so that if they need to reach you about an urgent matter, they'll know why you're not electronically reachable. If necessary, provide children and others who may need to reach you with an emergency contact person on your "dry" days. Confirm with your backup person that they will be available.

Day 23. Commit to going tech-free on your next vacation, except when a specific matter, perhaps work related, absolutely requires tech access.

Day 24. Refrain from using while interacting with your children. If you don't have children, refrain from use while with your pets (or plants).

Day 25. Take a half-hour tech-free walk with no destination. Wander like a happy dog.

Day 26. Spend 10 minutes doing nothing — on purpose. Sit still, be quiet, listen to the sounds, feel your breath, experience the sensations in your body.

Day 27. Send a handwritten letter, card or note to someone you know. Express anything that feels important about your detox.

Day 28. Do something in the "real" world that you would ordinarily do online — for example, call a friend instead of emailing or go to the store to buy food or a magazine or a book.

Day 29. Write down three things you are grateful for or happy about that are not tech-based.

Day 30. Make this moment matter, right now. Three times today, stop what you are doing and fully be where you are, sense your direct experience, allow things to be exactly as they are. Feel your own presence.

Off Your Screen and Into Your Body

As you decrease your use of technology, it will be helpful and important to add activities to your day that involve the body. Detoxing will free up a lot of energy that used to be directed toward your screens; this energy will need a place to land and be channeled. Moving your body is most useful for this purpose. It will help you anchor yourself in the physical and give your attention a new place to reside. In honor of your aspirations and actions, why not get up right now and give your recovery a shot of vitality? Move, dance, shake, rattle, roll, walk, stretch, swing, sway — do whatever your body longs to do. Feel and celebrate the freedom you are choosing to create! [76]

6. Proven Ways to Beat Addiction

Some therapists call these "addiction busters." Perhaps some of them will work for your family as they overcome the dependence on technology.

- Use the buddy system
  - Some programs call this person an "accountability partner." Choose someone who will ask you the hard questions ("Have you looked at pornography this week? Or "Let me see your screen usage numbers.") Choose a tough person—someone who will not let you slide.
  - Books can be buddies too. The right book can remind you to stay strong, and that the fight is worth the outcome. Maybe this book will serve in that capacity.

- Know your weak spots
  - Do you always play games on your phone right before bed? Do you wake up and immediately check your email or social

media? What areas are the toughest to give up? Whatever they are, you need to replace those habits with better, more productive ones. Perhaps a walk before bedtime with your spouse, or maybe an after-dinner walk while the kids ride their bikes instead of every member of the household gravitating to their individual electronic devices. Maybe a few minutes of stretching and time for an extra cup of coffee in the mornings since you are ignoring your phone.

- Move your body
  - o Movement and physical exertion are great ways to get the body out of the fight or flight (sympathetic) state and into the rest and digest (parasympathetic) state. How about a game of flashlight tag or a quick game of "horse" on the basketball court? Instead of staying on your laptop while the kids are at Karate lessons, why not take lessons yourself?

- Take up a hobby
  - o Remember hobbies? We rarely have time for them because our time is eaten up weeding through emails (unsubscribe!) and posting inane arguments about politics on social media. Do your children have hobbies? They should. Hobbies are a rich source of personal development and can ultimately lead to kids finding their calling in life.

- Write it down
  - o Keep a journal of how your life is changing, how your family is changing, how your time is being freed up. Write down your struggles, your triumphs and your discoveries. That's how this book started!

- Teach it to learn it
  - o The best way to learn something is to teach it to others. Share the ideas in this book with your small group/life group, with your neighbors or extended family members. Without being preachy, just share your experiences with detoxing off the

overuse of technology. By teaching others, you reinforce the concepts and the power of what you are accomplishing.

- Pray about it
    - o Yes, I know this should be first on the list, but let's be real. It's often NOT first on our list. Pray for grace to create a new normal in your home. Pray for grace as you conquer your own addiction to technology. Pray for grace for your children as they change the trajectories of their lives. Pray for the grace to remember that even though the struggle is real, it's worth it.

Questions to Ponder & Discuss

1. What digital curfew have you set for your family? Is this the right balance?
2. Do you have any family rituals at the dinner table? What are they? What is one you could start practicing?
3. Do you ask others to put their phone away when you are together? If not, will you start?
4. In what ways have you been creative in turning off devices, i.e., engaging more intentionally with others?
5. What steps can you take to reduce the amount of time you are on your devices? What about for your children?
6. Have you noticed a decrease in critical thinking over the years? Did you realize screens affected the cortex of the developing brain?
7. Why is it important to teach your children to balance their brains with indoor as well as outdoor activities?
8. Do you think you need to do a Digital Detox? Why or why not?
9. Do you have/need a digital accountability partner? Have you identified someone you can ask? And be one for?
10. What are your digital weak spots? What can you do to overcome them?

SIX

PHONE ETIQUETTE: A LOST ART

Technology came on fast and furious, full throttle—but now that we have seen its impact on our families, we need to take control of it PRONTO! We need to teach our children and young adults that it is rude and unacceptable to stop a conversation to look at a text message. Unless one has prefaced the conversation with the fact that he is waiting for a response or expecting an important phone call, this breach of good behavior should not happen. We teach this phone etiquette to our children the same way we teach them everything else—a combination of example, reward and consequences, repetition, and consistency. It may not be easy, but it's just that simple.

We teach them to use the toilet, to read, to drive, to behave in church or at a restaurant, to add and subtract, multiply and divide—to do *anything* by showing the example of how to behave, by laying out the rules (boundaries) in accordance with what is going to make them succeed and what is going to make them have troubles. We set the boundary to further progress them towards the goal of succeeding. In the last chapter we laid out what, in my experience, has been the overwhelming goal of most parents: that their children become the <u>best</u> version of themselves that they can possibly be—fully human, and yet reflecting the divine.

So, what does all that have to do with phone etiquette? And what is phone etiquette anyway? Does anyone still use the word *etiquette*? After all, the word was coined in 1750. Does it still apply to modern society? (spoiler alert: the answer is yes.) In fact, the ruder, more populated, and less civilized this world gets, the more we need formal rules of conduct for how people should behave. Less personal space means more responsibility for everyone to respect the boundaries of others. That's the thing about good manners (or etiquette)—it isn't a set of antiquated rules to keep the upper crust lording it over the working class. Instead, the focus of good manners, etiquette, or polite behavior is honoring the other persons around you by putting their needs above your own—or at least equal to your own.

Think through your day. Were others considerate of your personal space? Your time? Your feelings? Your health and well-being? What would your day have been like if everyone you encountered had treated you with honor and politeness? How about you—were you polite and considerate of others during your day? Did you allow someone to go ahead of you in line or in traffic? Did you speak kind words? Smile at others in your vicinity? Pick up something that was dropped by another? Allowed someone a seat while you stood? Give someone your full, undivided attention? These are all ways you can show honor to others and put their needs at least equal with your own.[77]

Since phone etiquette is a lost art, let's take a trip down memory lane. The Bell Telephone Service distributed a booklet back in the 1950s to teach children how to use the phone, and to teach them the etiquette necessary for carrying on a polite phone conversation. Why did they have to do this? Because in the previous decade, about 2/3 of Americans did not even have access to a telephone in their homes![78] This was new technology, and it called for a defining of the rules of good manners. Here are some of the rules of telephone etiquette taught[79] (see how many would still apply today!):

- You do not have to shout. Speak as though the other person were in the same room. (Ever been in a grocery store where the husband has his wife on speaker phone because he can't find something?)
- Speak in a natural, clear voice. ('Sup?)
- If the person you are calling does not answer right away, let the telephone ring at least a minute. He or she may be in another part of the house or outdoors. (leaves a rude voicemail because he can't get you right away)
- When you are calling someone and you get the busy signal, hang up right away and wait for several minutes before calling again.

- When you telephone, the other person cannot see you. He judges you by your voice. (Are we distracted with ten other things while talking to another on the phone?)
- Be natural and polite when using the telephone and you will make a good impression.
- If you call the wrong number, apologize to the person who answers.
- Be polite if someone calls your number by mistake. ("Who dis?")
- Don't hog the line making call after call. Others need to make calls too.
- Your conversation will be more personal if you speak TO the person at the other end of the line rather than AT the telephone. (Ever see someone shouting at her phone?)
- End the call gracefully. Be sure to thank the other person if he has been helpful and say "good-bye" so he will know you have finished. And as a parting, thoughtful gesture, please hang up gently.
- Answer calls promptly.
- Be brief when you call another, being respectful of their time. ("Whatcha' doing?")
- Use the other person's name when talking over the phone. ("Yo!")
- Give all your attention. Listen carefully and politely to the other person and interrupt only if necessary. Good manners apply to telephone conversations as well as face-to-face contacts.
- Be helpful and tactful.
- Think of the telephone as a doorway. Others will judge you by the welcome they receive and the helpfulness of your telephone attitude.[80]

New technology calls for new rules. But where are the rules written about how to behave while texting, talking on a mobile device, or tweeting? Do good manners even matter in the digital world? If so, where are they being practiced? If not, then why not? In his now decades old book, Robert Fulghum reminds us that everything we need to know we learned in Kindergarten.[81] The Golden Rule, love, basic sanitation, ecology, politics, equality, and sane living. Good manners. Saying please and thank you. Making eye contact when someone is speaking. Shaking hands firmly and politely. Not interrupting. Not hitting. Not being rude. Using indoor voices. Not having a potty mouth. Paying attention. Listening without fidgeting. If you can't say something nice, don't say anything at all. What would our world look like if we practiced these simple rules of etiquette today?

To be fair, most of us don't realize we are being rude. We act as if pleasantries are a thing of the past, but the guidelines of good manners exist even in the face of changing technology. We've all been there having a pleasant conversation with someone when they stopped abruptly, sneaked a look at their phone, and the moment is gone. We just stand there—not putting the word "rude" to the behavior—our silence granting consent. Back in the day, we were sent to school to be civilized—to be introduced to the essential machinery of human society. To become good citizens and neighbors. We were sent to school because society at large judged it so essential that we be educated that we were forced to attend school by law. There we were taught the basic principles upon which civilization rests. There was no other way. The ones who didn't learn these rudimentary lessons were "held back" or they eventually dropped out. According to Fulghum, from the first day of school we are taught in words understandable to us rules that are universal—rules that have come to be prized as "the foundation of community and culture."[82] Though kids only know them as "classroom rules," they are in fact the distillation of all the composite wisdom of generations as to what works in society and what doesn't—or shouldn't. There is much going on in society today that should not be happening.

Now schools often resemble jungles where the most ferocious and least caring members rule. Teachers are overwhelmed and often afraid. Principals don't back them for fear of a lawsuit, and parents don't back them because the *cult of youth* is strong and insinuates that teachers don't really know any better than the students or that the teachers have no more rights than the kids do. This attitude (whether conscious or subconscious) leads to a great deal of disrespect towards authority (i.e. teachers) by children. In the last several years I have started substitute teaching in a local school, and I am amazed at the lack of respect students have for teachers and others in authority. I went in thinking that the rule of "no phones during class" would be understood and universally applied. Sadly, it is not. Teachers themselves make that decision for their classrooms, and even if they say "no phones," students often do not comply. I went in determined to enforce this simple rule so that students could concentrate and actually learn something.

After discussing the school's policy on cell phone usage in the classroom, recently I told a 9th grade class of students they were not allowed phones during the class period. As I walked around, I was shocked at how many had their phones out for various reasons. I gave them an ultimatum if phones came out then they would be taken away. As I walked around the classroom, a young man was on his phone changing his music selection. Shocking. I was standing in the front of the room, a young lady pulled out her phone and did the usual sideways phone hold pose for Snapchat. I could not believe it, but what happened next left me speechless. The young lady next to her took *her* phone out and put it on her desk, the one who had just taken a Snapchat picture looked at her friend and called her out for having her phone. I looked at her, shocked. I asked if she realized I had seen her take a Snapchat picture, and she looked back at me as though I had grown ten heads, with an expression saying, "Really?" as if to say, "You saw that?" Surreal! There are times I have to remind myself that I am in a classroom not romper room.

Unfortunately for the students, I am hoping to make a change with phone usage in the classroom so they are the unlucky ones to get a substitute who will actually hold her standard, no phones unless allowed by the teacher. I am learning to be very prescriptive when I address my phone usage in the classroom. Most often, students say, "Our teacher lets us use our phones." I have asked Administration to have the teachers write in their substitute folder what their individual policy is for each class since it is no longer a school policy but by teacher. Well I told the students, phones are not to be used. None on the desk, no music since they will inevitably have to take their phone out to change songs, no phones are to be used. I was very clear. No one should be using phones during class time. Throughout the class period, as I roamed around, I confiscated seven phones. It is mind blowing! As I took one phone, I reminded them that phones are not to be in use. Then another and another. If you can believe it, they were annoyed that their phones were taken even though I had told them phones were not to be used during class. It boggles my mind, but it demonstrates to me the lack of respect young people have now for those in authority or otherwise.

I have taught some of the students previously, so this was not new to them. They just did not care. I am fortunate. I leave the classroom and choose if I want to go back. What about the teacher who has to deal with this day in and day out? No wonder they are drained and quitting in record numbers.[83] Before I started substituting, I wondered why classrooms allowed phones. Now I know. The teachers and administrators are worn down. Some teachers ask themselves every day if what they are doing is worth the trouble. What can *we* do to make a difference? I do not believe phones are necessary in the classroom. Remember what we have learned: if there is an emergency, you will not be able to reach your child because all phone lines will be jammed. We need to support teachers and administrators to uphold this very common-sense rule of no phones during class time.

Parents are sometimes more worried about their child's self-esteem than they are about their etiquette. This is a shame because true self-esteem doesn't come from getting one's way. Nor does it come from someone telling us we are special. No one can *give* another person self-esteem. It is earned by achieving age-appropriate or stage appropriate benchmarks. It is achieved by accomplishing after hard work what we couldn't accomplish just a short time ago. We feel good when we can color in the lines, when we can write cursive, when we can shoot a layup, do a set of pushups, or when we earn good grades. This whole concept has been diminished and twisted. The lost art of phone etiquette is a mirror of the loss of other forms of etiquette in society. The misuse and overuse of technology has made us a nation of impatient, rude, demanding, childish humans—tweeting out any mean, indecent thing we have an urge to communicate without any self-restraint.

Kids haven't been taught phone etiquette because this new technology didn't come with a rule book, and most parents haven't invested the time to teach the young ones how to act with a powerful tool in their hands. In all transparency, I didn't invest in it either! We didn't know what we didn't know! But now we do. The phone on the wall with the ten-foot twisty cord was so simple compared to phones today. In a split second, kids can copy an embarrassing picture or a private text or email and send it to everyone they know to ridicule another child. This kind of power in the hands of little people who don't even have a fully functional frontal lobe is terrifying!

Of course, it's not just kids who suffer. Think about all the phone videos that have gone viral making fun of others. None of us ever wants to be caught mid-rant, but the fact is we are all imperfect human beings doing the best we can. Our privacy should be respected, but we all know it won't be with the availability of cameras on cell phones. Videos have surfaced of teens just being teens, but those videos have sometimes cost those kids a job or even a college scholarship. Someone had to share that information with the general public. It may have even been a "friend!" Recently I went to a wedding in Rochester, New York. A groomsman told me a sad story about one of his good friends who was a police officer. This friend had made a clean arrest of a man who was clearly breaking the law; however, someone shot a video of the transaction with a cell phone and posted it on Facebook. Unfortunately, this upstanding police officer was not supported by his commander, and due to the backlash from social media, he quit the police force. It just wasn't worth putting his life on the line daily to have a bunch of Facebook groupies be both judge and jury. This type of situation is a zero-sum game. No one wins. The country is now without many good teachers, police officers, and others because of the emotional overreactions to video clips taken out of context and broadcast to millions who are not even remotely involved in the situation. By sharing these types of things on social media sites, we are inviting unsolicited opinions and responses by those not involved, those hiding behind a computer screen, those who have nothing to lose by showing their worst selves. They have no skin in the game.

When one family tries to take a stand and denies the early access of phones and other related gadgets to their children, it can feel like torture for those children. They are bullied, teased, or left out because they don't share the common tool—the phone. This shouldn't make us want to go out and buy them a phone! It should make us mad enough to do something about it. If you are a parent who has chosen to give your child a phone, then at least teach them to include those who choose not to. That is the kind of thing we learned in Kindergarten. Teach them.

A friend of mine is in the thick of this quandary right now. Her daughter is turning twelve, and she is thinking of giving her a phone with text and talk capability. Over the last couple of years, the other girls in the neighborhood have all received cell phones, while she didn't have one. In a sane world, this should not pose a problem, but in our world today, it did. She was often skipped over when the girls in the neighborhood got together. Her friends sometimes forgot she even existed because she wasn't constantly interacting with them on the phone and on social media. Once when she did get invited to hang out, one of the 11-year-olds (!) was making a tiktok video. The daughter of my friend tried to get into the video—join in the fun. She was told in no uncertain terms that she wasn't allowed into the video. The reason? "You don't have the following I have." If this doesn't make your blood boil, I don't know what would. A following? At eleven years old? What have we come to? These children should have been taught to include all friends whether they own a phone or not. In another instance with the same group of girls, they were having a night out when my friend's daughter found herself forced to sit out alone away from the group because she just didn't fit in with the phone-owning, pre-pubescent girls with the huge "followings." This type of ostracization can scar a young person for life. Please, teach your children about this.

Teach them to:

- Not look at the phone with every ding! In fact, teach them to turn off notifications. Make it a rule and keep that rule for yourself. Whatever it is, it will wait, and it's not as important as the actual people you are with in the moment.
- Turn off their phones during school hours or when they are at work. Don't text them while they are at school or work. That just makes the problem worse!
- Be kind on social media if they are going to use it.
- Be accountable for what they post, and what they text—especially younger teens. Teach them never to text or post anything they wouldn't say in front of their parents. Back this up with regular checks of their stuff.
- Include those who don't have phones. Don't make fun of them. Don't exclude them.

- Avoid looking at their phones when already engaged in a face-to-face conversation.
- Not take calls in public unless they absolutely can't avoid doing so.
- Not to text or talk and drive! With many cars having hands-free devices to receive phone calls, it's still important to know that the available studies so far suggest that talking on the phone while driving, even hands-free is as bad or worse than driving drunk.[84] According to the National Safety Council, 24 percent of all car crashes involve cell phone conversations.
- Not to be that person who looks things up on Google during a conversation to prove the other person wrong. Curiosity is not a virtue when it is ruled by impatience.
- Not to put someone on speaker phone where others can hear the conversation unless the person who is talking is informed that they are being heard by others. Not to do so is unfair and potentially harmful and embarrassing to the speaker.

The Emily Post Institute includes these *specific* rules of etiquette for all who are talking and texting on cell phones:

- Be in control of your phone, don't let it control you!
- Speak softly.
- Be courteous to those you are with; turn off your phone if it will be interrupting a conversation or activity.
- Watch your language. Keep it clean, especially when others can overhear you.
- Avoid talking about personal or confidential topics in a public place.
- If it must be on and it could bother others, use the "silent" mode and move away to talk.
- Don't make calls in a library, theater, church, or from your table in a restaurant.
- Don't text to inform someone of sad news or to end a relationship. Deliver the news in person or by phone.
- Be aware—not everyone has unlimited texting as part of their service plan.

- Keep your text messages brief. If it runs on and on, make a phone call instead.
- Be careful when choosing a recipient from your phone book; a slip of the finger could send the text to a wrong recipient.
- When you text someone who doesn't have your number, start by stating who you are.
- If you receive a text by mistake, respond to the sender with "Sorry, wrong number."
- Don't text at the movies, a play, or a concert—the screen light is annoying to others.
- Don't text anything confidential, private, or potentially embarrassing. It may be forwarded which could be potentially embarrassing or hurtful to you or others.
- Don't be upset if your text doesn't get an immediate response—you can't know for sure when the recipient will read the message.
- Don't answer the phone, make phone calls, or text others while in the bathroom.
- Just as you shouldn't answer your phone during a conversation, you shouldn't text when you're engaged with someone else. If you are with someone who won't stop texting during your conversation, feel free to excuse yourself until they have concluded their messaging.

It may be a good idea to take one of these rules each week and make it a topic of family discussion. Write the rule on the kitchen chalkboard, or on post-it notes around the house. Work on the rule as a family with consequences for breaking the rule—like a jar where a certain dollar value "fine" is put in when the rule is broken. It is not enough to read, understand, or even memorize these rules of *netiquette*. We must teach them to our children. Schools aren't doing it, so parents have to train their children how to be good citizens, good neighbors, good human beings. At the core of this concept is simply the humility to put another before ourselves. Biblical concept—but not popular. The Bible has a bit to say about good manners:

- Luke 6:31 Do to others as you would have them do to you.

- 1 Corinthians 15:33 Do not be misled: "Bad company corrupts good character."
- 1 Peter 3:8 Finally, all of you, be like-minded, be sympathetic, love one another, be compassionate and humble.
- Ephesians 4:29 Do not let any unwholesome talk come out of your mouths, but only what is helpful for building others up according to their needs, that it may benefit those who listen.
- Romans 12:10 Be devoted to one another in love. Honor one another above yourselves.
- Philippians 2:3 Do nothing out of selfish ambition or vain conceit. Rather in humility value others above yourselves.
- 1 Corinthians 13:4-5 Love is patient, love is kind. It does not envy, it does not boast, it is not proud. It does not dishonor others, it is not self-seeking, it is not easily angered, it keeps no record of wrongs.
- Colossians 4:6 Let your conversation be always full of grace, seasoned with salt, so that you may know how to answer everyone.
- Titus 3:1-2 Remind the people to...be ready to do whatever is good, to slander no one, to be peaceable and considerate, and always to be gently toward everyone.
- 1 Corinthians 14:40 But everything should be done in a fitting and orderly way.

For our purposes here, this may be the most important verse: "Train up a child in the way he should go; even when he is old, he will not depart from it."[85] As we train our children in matters of humility, patience, honor, and the good manners that put shoe leather to these lofty but attainable character qualities, may we always know that our labor is not in vain. Even when they are old, our children will follow the path we have laid out for them—be that a good path of etiquette that treats others with honor and leads to fully functional adulthood, or not. The choice is ours. If you take anything away from this book, let it be this: Technology is a useful servant but a dangerous master.[86]

Questions to Ponder & Discuss

1. How have you taught your children phone etiquette? What about digital device etiquette? Did you realize there is a difference?
2. Do you think it is still necessary? Why or why not?
3. Is it just teenagers that lack phone etiquette or have you seen it displayed in adults as well?
4. Who do you think should teach digital phone etiquette?
5. Is it rude if you are engaged in a face-to-face conversation, and someone looks at their device?
6. What is your child's school policy on phones in the classroom? Should it be teacher dictated or district mandated?
7. Were you aware how distracting phones can be in the classroom even if there is a no phones policy?
8. Were you aware students listened to music on their devices during class time? Do you think it is a good idea?
9. If your child has a phone, have you purposely taught them to include others who do not yet have a phone/device?
10. Will you teach them digital phone etiquette if you have not already done so? Why or why not?

SEVEN

7 THINGS YOU CAN GIVE YOUR KIDS THAT TECHNOLOGY CAN'T

"Where is the Life we have lost in living? Where is
the wisdom we have lost in knowledge?
Where is the knowledge we have lost in information?" --T.S. Eliot

Wisdom: Connection to Truth

A pastor once told me the difference between knowledge and wisdom, and I never forgot it. He said that knowledge tells us that a tomato is a fruit, but wisdom tells us not to put it into a fruit salad! Although it's silly, it's true! Google or Reddit can give our children knowledge and facts, but only parents, teachers, spiritual leaders, and grandparents can relate those facts to real-life context and eternal values! Facts plus experience equals knowledge. Knowledge plus reverence equals wisdom. The fear of the Lord is the beginning of wisdom—it starts with the reverence that realizes there is something bigger and wiser than us.[87] In that regard, we as parents need to be careful that we aren't letting our children be raised by Google or any other algorithm-based digital platform.

Awe can be inspired by observing man-made, technological feats such as the Space Shuttle or the Brooklyn Bridge, but true reverence can only be stirred when we as humans are in the presence of something bigger than the human experience—forces stronger than any man or woman. In order to develop this type of reverence in our children, we must slow down *and slow them down* long enough to notice. Take them to the porch to watch a violent thunderstorm replete with wind, rain, and lightning. Take them to the Grand Canyon and just look at the majesty—no headphones or portable video games. Teach them to grow their own flowers and food—even if it's just sprouting seeds in a cup in a sunny window. Let them watch a litter of puppies or kittens being born. Expose them to nature and teach them reverence. It will serve them well in the long run.

Some writers explain the need for reverence this way:

- Power without reverence is aflame with arrogance, while service without reverence is smoldering toward rebellion.
- Politics without reverence is blind to the general good and deaf to advice from people who are powerless.
- Reverence kindles warmth in friendship and family life. And because without reverence, things fall apart. People do not know how to respect each other and themselves.
- Without reverence, a house is not a home, a boss is not a leader, an instructor is not a teacher.
- We must abandon arrogance and stand in awe. We must recover the sense of the majesty of creation, and the ability to be worshipful in its presence.
- Reverence keeps technology in its place.
- Reverence unlocks beauty in our lives because what you encounter, recognize or discover depends to a large degree on the quality of your approach. When we approach with reverence, great things decide to approach us.
- Reverence invites us to pay attention.

We teach children reverence by example and by helping them interpret the world around them. We teach them that words are vessels, and they can be filled with light or with darkness—that what they think, say, and do matters for eternity. Then we teach them the true objects of reverence—just things, true things, pure things, good things, things of good reputation, things that are lovely, worthy and weighty—things that aren't vain and empty.[88] This happens intentionally and consciously. Parents, grandparents, aunts, uncles, older siblings, and teachers all play an irreplaceable role in cultivating reverent hearts and a taste for what is worthy. Technology is now and always will be unable to accomplish this.

Nature: Connection to our Planet

One way to build reverence and cultivate wonder in our children is by letting them explore nature daily. The study of nature provokes humility in children and adults. Americans in the Boomer generation (1946-1964) enjoyed a type of free and natural play outdoors that is unheard of today. They threw frisbees on the lawn, lay down on grassy slopes and watched the clouds move overhead, roller skated and biked on the streets and sidewalks, and learned high level negotiation skills when playing pickup baseball or basketball games with other children. They learned to build treehouses, dig holes, and make rope swings. They swam in any body of water they could find. This type of play seems like a "quaint artifact" in today's world of Fortnight, Minecraft, YouTube and TikTok.

Most kids today don't even know how to conduct a simple "eenie, meenie, miny, moe" that was the basis of choosing who's "it" for decades! Kids today don't know how to play unless that play is electronic or highly organized and controlled by others. Most, if not all play today is membership based and expensive. Swim team, travel baseball and soccer, cheerleading, gymnastics, trampoline parks, play dates, theme parks, and water slides. Without constant supervision, kids say they are bored and don't know how to entertain themselves. One fourth grade student in San Diego put it this way: "I like to play indoors better 'cause that's where all the electrical outlets are."[89]

Because of this, children have lost their sense of *wonder* and their sense of *wander*. They are not allowed enough time to *wonder* about anything—seeking an immediate answer from the oracle Google or cathedrals of pooled ignorance like Reddit and Quora, and they are not allowed enough space to *wander* because parents have been convinced that danger is lurking in nature around every shrub and bush. Swim in a pond without chlorine? How barbaric! Parents have made children afraid of going out in the sun without being slathered in sunscreen even though the chemicals in most sunscreens are detrimental to health.[90] Most Americans show vitamin D deficiency—a problem easily remedied by regular exposure without sunscreen to the sun. Kids are taught to be afraid of ticks and bugs and are told to wear chemical-laden bug repellant. They are coached often by parents and teachers about "stranger-danger" (which is a clear and present threat) but statistically, the largest percentage of child-victimizations occur from extended family and acquaintances—not strangers![91]

Kids today believe that the polar bears are dying because of global warming, but few of them have seen a glacier or a polar bear in real life outside of a zoo. Many teens dabble in being vegan or vegetarian, while they have never actually grown a vegetable in their lives and don't have a real solid idea about where their food originates or what process it goes through before it gets to their plates. Most of them would be shocked to know that their vegetables are fertilized with animal poo, and how those nutrients become part of the amazing food chain that sustains them.

> *"Unlike television, nature does not steal time; it amplifies it."*
> --Richard Louv

Children have been taught by the dominant cultural narrative to believe that nature equals doom, even though several studies suggest that the intentional and regular exposure of children to nature is a powerful type of therapy for ADD/ADHD, anxiety, and other mental and social issues.[92] Researchers tell us that time in natural settings (away from the city) is helpful for increasing attention span and diminishing impulsivity. Whether it's a backyard, school playground, city park, or an outcropping of trees in the suburban neighborhood, behavior improves when children have adequate green time. What is adequate? Well, let's start with the same amount of time they are playing video games or staring at their phones. Our mental, physical, emotional, and spiritual health depend on regular contact and communion with nature.

This is something we can provide for our children that no amount of engagement with digital technology can provide. We need to be intentional about taking kids out in nature and helping them explore the wonders there. Sending them to summer camp is not enough!

God shows up in nature. We see a beautiful word picture of natural revelation in Psalm 19:

The heavens declare the glory of God; the skies proclaim the work of his hands. Day after day they pour forth speech night after night, they reveal knowledge. They have no speech; they use no words; no sound is heard from them. Yet their voice goes out into all the earth, their words to the ends of the world. In the heavens God has pitched a tent for the sun. It is like a bridegroom coming out of his chamber, like a champion rejoicing to run his course. It rises at one end of the heavens and makes its circuit to the other; nothing is deprived of its warmth.

When was the last time you saw your child look up in wonder at the sky, or study a blade of grass, or watch a hawk in flight? When was the last time you saw awe in her eyes at the beauty of a field of wildflowers? When was the last time you experienced that yourself?

Belonging: Connection to Family and Community

Once a child has developed a reverent heart and learned to appreciate and enjoy nature, only then is he or she ready to truly appreciate connection with family and community. A reverent heart does no harm, and it realizes the intricate web of connection that constitutes the different communities we live and thrive in—church, neighborhood, teams, school, city, town, country, world. The type of "belonging" that is promised by social media and by online gaming communities is a *false belonging*. Most social media markers of belonging and acceptance are based on whether the user is like other users—a clone—not daring to be different. Because in general, humans hate what they fear, and fear what they do not understand, there is an enormous amount of cyberbullying that goes on in the world of Facebook, Twitter, and Instagram. And if you have ever heard a twelve-year-old playing online video games with his friends, you quickly realized that this trash-talking, bullying, obnoxious behavior is not something you really wish your child to emulate or even participate in. If you heard it, would you stop it? DID you stop it?

It's hard to say which came first—a need for belonging that wasn't being met or the false belonging of online communities that filled the void. What we do know is that belonging is one of the basic needs of the human heart, and loneliness is epidemic among teens and even tweens right now. Forty percent of 16-24-year-olds say they are lonely <u>often or very often</u>. This according to the largest survey of its kind in 2018. The Office for National Statistics and The Children's Society collaborated on this research as well, and they concluded that the online world is one reason for this overwhelming loneliness in kids.[93] This online world exerts a huge influence on how kids interact with others (digitally, not in person) and how they experience their world. Comparing themselves (their looks, popularity, and experiences) to images of others online plays into this a great deal.

How do you know if your child is lonely? Being alone doesn't automatically equate to loneliness. You have undoubtedly experienced at one time or another being in a crowd and feeling utterly alone or being alone and being perfectly content. These days are different though. The social and political response to the coronavirus has been massive lockdowns, quarantine for healthy individuals, mass closings of churches and schools, and pressure to "stay home and stay safe." Besides the tremendous economic upheaval this has caused, the massive numbers of small businesses who couldn't survive the shutdowns, and the millions of unemployed, there exists the loneliness issue. Humans are not hardwired for social isolation. Being social is our jam, and it always has been. For kids and teens, this upheaval to their academic year, their social lives, their church lives, and their home lives has been nothing short of catastrophic.

Even before the pandemic, public health officials were concerned about the "epidemic of loneliness" in the United States. The measures taken by the powers that be to shut normally healthy and productive citizens up in their homes and forbidding them to visit relatives and friends has made the loneliness epidemic far worse. For 35.7 million Americans who live alone, that means no meaningful social contact at all, potentially for months on end. Adults can see the "light at the end of the tunnel," but children don't have that kind of abstract reasoning. In their world, this isolation will go on forever and they have no power to do anything about it.[94] We don't know where the tipping point will be when acute loneliness transitions into a chronic condition with long-term consequences. Parents face some of the same questions they faced before, but the stakes are so much higher now. "Did my child become depressed because he was lonely? Or did he become isolated because he was depressed? Are they withdrawn out of fear? Boredom? Loneliness? Has increased use of social media made them more depressed and lonelier? Research shows that loneliness *may subside* for teens and younger adults when they reduce their social media usage.[95]

Children and teens are very good at hiding their feelings, so you may not notice that something is wrong unless you work at finding out. Often, we will ask a teen *directly* about his feelings as we would a young child. It doesn't take long to find out that most teens don't open up to that approach, rather seeing it as an intrusion into the private world they are desperately trying to create. Some good advice I got from a successful mother of four was that it's best to talk deeply to young children while they are in the bathtub, preteens and younger teens while driving in the car alone with them, and older teens in a restaurant of their choosing. Some signs[96] your teenager is lonely:

- Low self-esteem and loss of confidence
- Sadness, withdrawal, and pulling away from the family or former friends
- Excessive anger or acting out
- No interest in trying new things or engaging in social activities
- No interest in hobbies or pursuits they formerly enjoyed
- Risky behaviors (drinking, drugs, smoking, sex) to gain peer acceptance

In times past, several generations of family lived in the same house, or at least the same neighborhood. Children often went to the same schools their parents did, and there was continuity and community in smaller towns or in small neighborhoods in big cities. Today grandparents often live far away. Families are smaller, siblings and cousins are fewer. It will take effort to create for your children a sense of community and family in this current climate. The church also used to be a source of community, but huge megachurches make it hard for some families to connect unless they are actively part of a small group. By adopting "family members" from your faith community or neighborhood, you can create a web of connection that will provide an alternative world—a REAL world of love and support that your teens so desperately need—whether they express it or not.

Another good way to create belonging is by rituals and traditions. Our future is not shaped by big events or decisions. The little things we do ritualistically every day are what determine our future, and those little things are what kids remember when they are grown. Waking children up the same way every morning—maybe with the same words or the same silly song, saying a blessing before every dinner meal, birthday rituals, holiday rituals, daily rituals, weekly rituals like attending church on Sundays or ice cream after school on Fridays—the more you keep these simple but sacred routines constant, the stronger the imprint of memory will be for your children. Rituals increase our satisfaction in life because they add joy and meaning—a framework for our memories. Whenever an event engages the emotions, it makes for a stronger memory. So even if the kids are rolling their eyes and groaning at your "dad jokes" or howling for you to stop singing the same song to wake them with, keep doing these little rituals each day. You are depositing into the memory bank for future withdrawals.

Culture: Connection to Social and Moral Values

Online culture has very different values than the ones you want to cultivate in your children. Whether it is sitcoms on television, Disney movies, or YouTube videos, the culture that surrounds us is pagan. How many Disney movies have witches casting spells or show other pagan practices? How many portray disobedient behavior to parents with no real consequence but happily ever after? In the end, Hannah Montana came in "like a wrecking ball."[97] If you don't know what that last statement means, ask your kids. They'll know. When the Israelites were wandering their way to the promised land, they encountered some very wicked pagan practices including idol worship, child-sacrifice, and temple prostitution. The contrast between the prideful violence and sexual deviancy of the culture around them with the Torah's demands for honesty, humility, and holiness was stark. It was hard to imagine that the nation of Israel would succumb to these values so antithetical to their own. God knew differently. He commanded them not to study idols or bring them into their homes lest their sensibilities be corrupted. In fact, He commanded them to utterly detest idols and utterly abhor them because when even the most vulgar influences pass into the home, those influences grow less offensive and shocking daily, and more acceptable over time. The home is not just a building. It is the center of the child's world, and the heart of the family. When cultivating your values into your children (it has only been in the last generation that voices have questioned the right and responsibility of parents to do so), you don't need the online or digital world to undermine those very values. Look and listen to what your kids are being exposed to on a regular basis through the media:

- Alcohol/Drug use and abuse (Titus 2:6)
- Violence (James 3:17)
- Love of money (Hebrews 13:5)
- Prideful or spiteful behavior that is rewarded or unpunished (Proverbs 8:13)
- Crass commercialism (appeals to possession, pride, and power-seeking) (1 John 2:15-17)
- Immodest behavior and dress (1 Timothy 2:9)
- Sexual connotation or inuendo (Ephesians 5:4)
- Consumption of addictive, non-nutritive, unhealthy foods (1 Corinthians 6:19)
- Promiscuity involving same sex or opposite sex partners (1 Corinthians 6:18)
- Portrayal of people of faith as hypocrites, uneducated, superstitious, etc. (Isaiah 5:20)

And examine the medium itself. Studies since 1962 have been warning us that screen time (back then it was only television and cinema) is directly connected to impaired academic achievement.[98] There is no murky water here. The more a student watches images flickering across a screen, the worse he does in school. Period. The reasons for this are:

- Time—the more time on the screen, the less time studying or reading.

- Sleepiness—the more time on the screen, the worse the quality of sleep (wired but tired), and kids were sleepier the next day at school no matter when they went to bed.
- Flickering images—the quick cuts of digital stimulation and the flickering images alleviate the need for watchers to concentrate. That's why so many people watch TV to relax. The work of Harvard Professor T. Berry Brazelton showed that newborn babies who were hooked up to brain monitors and then exposed to a flickering light source (similar to television but with no pictures), stopped crying about fifteen minutes into exposure, and their brains produced alpha wave sleep patterns.
- Pace—the loud noises and fast pace of video games, videos, and television all suppress impulse control and make it harder to pay attention to the slow pace of the school classroom.
- Imagination—one Surgeon General's report of fourth, fifth, and sixth graders showed that watching television shows (cartoons or educational) depressed the students' creativity scores.[99] When we read we must conjure up images. Reading stirs and strengthens our imaginative capabilities. When we watch television, we are provided all the images. We don't have to work at it.

With all the hard work you put into cultivating right values in your children, you don't need the online world undermining those values and destroying through the medium or content what you are trying to create. Digital media can become the strongest voice in your child's life if you allow it to be.

Faith: Connection to God

We as humans carry what is called *imago Dei*—the image and likeness of God directly coded into our DNA. From the first humans who sacrificed animals to God or worshipped the Divine as they looked into the heavens, something in us has always sensed that there is more to life than the material world around us. God is mysterious and powerful—transcending human imagery. What we see is merely a cloudy version of the reality of God, but it will not always be so.[100]

As parents, grandparents, siblings, coaches, and teachers we have the unique ability and responsibility to show children how to connect to God—even if the images we use are cloudy and imperfect. In our world today we have removed holy language from our conversation. Even in many churches you won't find elevated language, dress, prayers, or symbolism. Many churches have abandoned these things so that they will seem "relatable" to the average person. One preacher put it this way: The modern church is addicted to big screens, skinny jeans, and fog machines![101] This is sad because our number one tool in navigating life's challenges throughout the centuries has always been prayer. We don't always appreciate how this lack of connection to God influences our thinking, decision making, and even our mental, emotional, and physical health! Without grace conveyed by the sacred language of prayer our souls will starve. At the end of the day, we are not merely a collection of dust and chemicals, flesh and bone; we are sacred beings who carry the image of God within us.

> *When we do not know what we believe in—*
> *when we are not empowered to*
> *Have an intimate, personal, conversational relationship with God—*
> *we are susceptible to believing the most potent voice in the room.*
> *Sometimes that voice comes carrying a darkness unimaginable.*[102]

Meaning: Connection to the Innate Worth of the Soul

This temporal, material world communicates most directly to your children through their use of technology. Think about that for a moment. These avenues of digital engagement are the primary messages they will carry with them into adulthood and beyond. What messages is technology sending to your kids about their innate worth and the meaning of life? I mean, after all, eternity isn't something for the future. Eternity is already here! We won't live a different life after we pass from these mortal bodies. We will live a different *kind* of life experience, but that life is our life now. We are already in eternal life. To flesh out this point, I bring in two men—not necessarily of the same Christian tradition that we are used to, but men who thought, spoke, and wrote prodigiously about the meaning that we give the lives that have been given to us.

"Everything can be taken from a man but one thing: the last of the human freedoms—to choose one's attitude in any given set of circumstances." Victor Frankl

Victor Frankl was a Jewish psychiatrist and neurologist from Austria who spent time in a concentration camp under Nazi domination during World War II. He discovered through this horrendous experience that the only thing that helped some of the prisoners survive was their understanding that their lives had meaning—that they were not living in vain. His book, *Man's Search for Meaning* was published in 1946 and it has been a best seller ever since. The way he saw it, people don't seek pleasure as their primary motivating force, but rather they seek endless pleasure and entertainment to numb themselves because they have been unable to find the meaning in their lives. Look around you. Everyone is using something or someone to get over something or someone. Addictions are rampant, and technology is just one of the many substances being abused. Frankl would argue that this is because the addicts don't believe or don't understand that everything they do and the way they do it has meaning. Victor Frankl believed that there are three components of a meaningful life:

1. To have a purpose that demands our attention and gets us out of bed every day to pursue it.
2. To be surrounded by people who love and accept us as we are—relationships and community.
3. To grow from overcoming life's challenges. That we use our challenges and sufferings to create something useful, or even something beneficial for others.

In other words, we bring meaning to our lives as we find our purpose amidst our pain. This brings us to our second man, Joseph Campbell. This American mythologist, writer and teacher also believed that we bring the meaning to our own lives. He advocated finding out what makes us truly joyful—not merely excited or thrilled, but deeply happy. He encouraged us to find out what that is and follow it at all costs. He called this process, *The Hero's Journey*. We see remnants of his teachings in silly movies like *City Slickers* where Billy Crystal learns from cowboy Jack Palance that the secret to life is to find "the one thing" and pursue it.[103] Joseph Campbell encourages readers not to seek meaning, but to seek the rapture of being alive. To create a life from which we need no vacation. In the words of the cowboy, to find the "one thing." Both men were coming from different perspectives and traditions, but both men taught that we must transcend the limited perspective of our individual circumstances and find what makes us truly alive, connected, authentic, and real. With a life like this, there is no need to watch television or escape into fantasy. Our life becomes our fantasy.

Purpose: Connection to Their Own Unique Assignment

For many years we have been taught by culture—even church culture—to find our life's purpose or our unique destiny. Evangelical churches usually prefer to focus on finding life's purpose, while apostolic churches paint the picture to members of a magnificent personal destiny to be filled. But God's call on your children's lives isn't about finding or filling—it's about following. Following the direction of God. Following the assignment given with the help of the Holy Spirit's guidance. It's a subtle difference but *finding one's purpose* is introspective—the church turned in on itself. An assignment is focused outward. Completing the task or mission is the only thing that matters. When a recruit joins the Marines, and the commanding officer asks, "Soldier, why are you here?" The answer is not "I'm here to find my purpose." The answer is "I'm here to receive my assignment." The Marine Corps has the purpose. Soldiers are on assignment. Parents, extended family members, teachers, youth workers, and coaches have the unique opportunity and responsibility to help children learn to listen to God and to be ready to carry out whatever assignments are given to them in their walk of faith. Along this same line, we can teach children how to influence the culture for Christ. Remember back from chapter one that another term for power is *influence*.

The most powerful assignment we have then is to carry out the purposes of Christ by influencing the culture we live in. This powerful assignment must be passed to the next generation if we want the Church to survive. When Jesus prayed for his disciples[104] he asked the Father not to take them out of the world, but to keep them from the evil one. Christians assimilate in culture, unlike several other religions. But Christians should be influencing the culture around them, not just blending in.

We are now at the end of the book, but this is only the beginning of the discussion about how families can rein in the misuse and overuse of technology that is robbing them of time (quality and quantity), talent (gifts used to bless others), touch (influence), tenderness (natural affection), and tenacity (frustration tolerance). It may seem like an overwhelming challenge to set up boundaries, put tools in place to manage technology usage, and teach basic digital device etiquette, but do remember that whatever God has called us to do, He will give us the grace to do it. It is only by the "common will" of many with one purpose that this will be accomplished.

So, he said to me, "This is the word of the Lord to Zerubbabel:
'Not by might nor by power, but by my
Spirit,' says the Lord Almighty." [105]

Questions to Ponder & Discuss

1. How are you developing reverence in your children? As a family what can you do?

2. As you reflect on the difference between knowledge and wisdom what struck you?

3. What is your children's favorite way to entertain themselves? Have they ever said they are bored? What do you do when that happens?

4. What non-organized activities do your children have? Can you think of any you can incorporate into their lives?

5. How much time do your children spend playing outside freely?

6. How many "friends" do your children have on social media? Are they real friends? Are they making lifelong friendships via social media?

7. Have you ever heard someone play online video games? What was it like? Was it pleasant to listen to? If not, did you try to curb this behavior?

8. Are your children lonely? Have low self-esteem? Sadness, withdrawal, excessive anger, risky anger? Have you asked? What did you say about their feelings? What could you say/do?

9. What family rituals do you have? Can you think of any new ones you can start?

10. Has technology/social media become an idol for you? Your children? What steps can you take to remove this idol?

11. Have you ever pondered what you were created to do? Explain.

12. How are you coming alongside your children to follow their God-given assignment?

13. We didn't know what we didn't know but now we do. This is a message of hope. Technology is not bad, but the misuse and overuse of it is a problem. Knowing this, what changes will you make to set up boundaries, put tools in place to manage proper device usage and teach proper digital etiquette?

AFTERWORD:
A CALL TO ACTION

I would be remiss if I didn't challenge you with a call to action. After all, social scientists tell us that knowledge without action can lead to depression. So many statistics and warnings. So much to think about, address, change, and accomplish. Like the Israelites standing at the threshold of the Promised Land, but discouraged by the giants, warriors, and obstacles to getting there, many of us can almost taste the sweetness of getting our families back. We can visualize and feel the warmth of returning affection and attention. But we pale. We fall back because the warriors are too strong, the giants are too scary, and the challenge is too great. We *know* that God is greater than all that is in the world, but we *feel,* and we *believe* that we are not up to the task. Yet we are commanded to muster that courage and exert our wills for good:

- *Be strong, and let us fight bravely for our people and the cities of our God. The Lord will do what is good in his sight. 1 Chronicles 19:13*
- *For God gave us a spirit not of fear but of power and love and self-control. 2 Tim. 1:7*
- *Wait for the Lord; be strong and let your heart take courage.... Psalm 27:14*
- *Trust in the Lord with all your heart, and do not lean on your own understanding. In all your ways acknowledge him, and he will make straight your paths. Proverbs 3:5-6*

What does it look like for you to muster courage in this moment? The first step is to commit to the Lord to change some things in your home. Shore up the boundaries, hold each other accountable, work together to protect the heart and soul of your family, and manage the monster of technology addiction. Treat this as a call from your heavenly Father to do things differently from here on out—one day at a time. To seal this commitment, you need to share it with someone you trust. Write that person's name here: _____

APPENDIX I

Safety Concerns

Some tips from Netsmartz.org for responding to cyberbullying:

- To keep others from using their email and Internet accounts, kids should never share Internet passwords with anyone other than parents, experts say.
- If children are harassed or bullied through instant messaging, help them use the "block" or "ban" feature to prevent the bully from contacting them.
- If a child keeps getting harassing emails, delete that email account and set up a new one.
- Remind your child to give the new email address only to family and a few trusted friends.
- Tell your child not to respond to rude or harassing emails, messages and postings. If the cyberbullying continues, call the police. Keep a record of the emails as proof.

Internet Safety Tips for Avoiding Cyberstalking and Predators

- Ask your children if they use a social networking site. Look at the site together or search for it yourself online. Social networking sites often have age limits. Some sites prohibit kids under 14 - but don't verify kids' ages, so anyone can use it. If you want to delete a site, work with your child to cancel the account, or contact the social networking site directly.

- Tell your kids not to post a full name, address, phone number, school name and other personal information that could help a stranger to find them. Remind them that photos - like your child in a team sweatshirt - can give away clues to where they live. Ask them not to send photos to people they meet online.
- Learn about privacy settings that allow kids to choose who can view their profiles. Explain that strangers who approach them online aren't always who they say they are - and that it's dangerous to meet them in real life. Tell them to "instant message" only with family or friends they already know off-line.
- When it comes to Internet safety, there's no substitute for parental supervision. Put your computer in a common area of your home, not a child's bedroom, so you can keep an eye on online activities. Go to websites that explain the short-hand kids use in instant messaging, like "POS" ("parent over shoulder") or "LMIRL" ("let's meet in real life"), so you know what's going on.
- Ask your kids to report any online sexual solicitation to you or another trusted adult right away. Shehan asks adults to report the event to the CyberTipline (800-843-5678), where staff will contact law enforcement agencies to investigate. He also advises parents to call their local police and save all offensive emails as evidence.

Internet Safety Tips for avoiding pornography

- Install Internet filtering software to block porn sites from any computer to which your child has access.
- Consider using filtering software that monitors and records instant messaging and chat room conversations, as well as websites visited.
- Consider using a monitoring program that filters pornography keywords in several languages. Why? Because some teens have figured out how to get around filters by typing in porn-related search terms in other languages

APPENDIX II

Resources

On Parental Controls:

Bark—https://www.bark.us/ Bark is an award-winning dashboard giving parents their time while building trust with their kids.

Forcefield—https://truth.best/spy-apps/forcefield-reviews/#what-is-forcefield-app

This is not a spying application. While developers were creating this app, they wanted to help parents and children collaborate in order to enable the highest level possible of cybersecurity and protection against Internet bullying. This is an easy-to-use and transparent tool intended to make the use of the Internet safer for your children. Due to a wide range of benefits and parental control feature, the Forcefield app attracts a huge audience of customers all over the world.

Net Nanny—https://www.netnanny.com/ios/#:~:text=Net%20Nanny%C2%AE%20for%20iOS%20provides%20the%20%231%2Drated%20parental,before%20it's%20viewed%20on%20websites.

Net Nanny for IOS provides the #1-rated parental control software to Apple devices, giving you visibility and control over your family's online experience. Net Nanny's parental control app for Apple devices lets you filter the Internet and block pornography before it is viewed on websites.

Circle—https://meetcircle.com/lp-2?utm_source=Google&utm_medium=SEM&utm_campaign=9610576554&utm_content=c-4308 49069407&utm_term=disney%20circle-e&gclid=EAIaIQobChMIk8-Q-4Gh6wIVzcDACh3siAYCEAAYASAAEgIuMfD_BwE

From mobile phones and tablets to smart TVs and video game consoles, Circle's parental controls let you set limits and filter content across every device, all from one central app.

Protect Young Eyes—https://protectyoungeyes.com/

The best internet safety information all in one place.

Axis—https://axis.org/ct/

Be equipped to have the lifelong conversation with: The Culture Translator Premium, Parent Guides, Conversation Kits, Expert Interviews, 10-day Teen Talks, Family Experiences, and more!

Covenant Eyes—https://www.covenanteyes.com/

Their accountability service helps participants overcome porn by monitoring screen activity and sending a report to a trusted ally who holds participants accountable for online choices.

On Slowing Down Your Family:

Bernadette Noll, *Slow Family Living: 75 Simple Ways to Slow Down, Connect, and Create More Joy.*

On Internet Pornography:

Books by Patrick Carnes: *Out of the Shadows* and *A Gentle Path*

Hooked: New Science on How Casual Sex is Affecting our Children by Joe S. Mcilhaney, Jr., MD and Freda McKissic Bush, MD

On Tech Overuse & Addiction:

Mary Aiken, *"The Cyber Effect—A Pioneering Cyberpsychologist Explains How Human Behavior Changes Online"* http://www.maryaiken.com/

Adam Alter, *"The Rise of Addictive Technology and the Business of Keeping Us Hooked"* and

"Irresistible" http://adamalterauthor.com/

Ryan Anderson, Ph.D., LMFT, MedFT, *"Navigating the Cyberscape: Evaluating and Improving Our Relationship with Smartphones, Social Media, Video Games, and the Internet."*

Hilda Burke, *The Phone Addiction Workbook: How to Identify Smartphone Dependency, Stop Compulsive Behavior and Develop a Healthy Relationship with Your Devices.*

Nicholas Carr, *"The Shallows: What the Internet is Doing to Our Brains"* and *"The Glass Cage: How Our Computers Are Changing Us,"* www.nicholascarr.com, blog: http://www.roughtype.com

Matthew Crawford, *"The World Beyond Your Head—On Becoming an Individual in the Age of Distraction,"* Institute for Advanced Studies in Culture, University of Virginia, https://www.thenewatlantis.com/authors/matthew-crawford

Anastasia Dedyukhina, PhD, *"Homo Distractus: Fight for your choices and identity in the digital age,"* Consciously Digital, https://www.consciously-digital.com/

Victoria Dunckley, *"Reset Your Child's Brain: A Four-Week Plan to End Meltdowns, Raise Grades, and Boost Social Skills by Reversing the Effects of Electronic Screen-Time"* https://drdunckley.com

Devora Heitner, *"Screenwise – Helping Kids Thrive and Survive in Their Digital World"* https://www.raisingdigitalnatives.com/

Nicholas Kardaras, PhD, *"Glow Kids: How Screen Addiction is Hijacking Our Kids – and How to Break the Trance:"* CEO, Omega Recovery and Maui Recovery; Starting *Launch House* in New York City Fall 2019. www.drkardaras.com

Andrew Keen, internet entrepreneur, Senior Fellow, CALinnovates and CNN columnist; Author of *"How to Fix The Future," "Cult of the Amateur: How The Internet Is Killing Our Culture," "Digital Vertigo: How Today's Social Revolution Is Dividing, Diminishing and Disorienting Us,"* and *"Internet is not the Answer."*

Jaron Lanier, Virtual reality expert and scholar at the interface between computer science and medicine, physics, and neuroscience. *Ten Arguments for Deleting Your Social Media Accounts Right Now," "Dawn of the New Everything: Encounters with Reality and Virtual Reality,"* and *"Who Owns the Future?"*

Daniel Levitin, Neuroscientist, Musician; *"The Organized Mind -Thinking Straight in the Age of Information Overload"* http://www.daniellevitin.org/

Professor David M. Levy, School of Information, University of Washington, and scholar in the transition from paper and print to digital; *"Mindful Tech: How to Bring Balance to Our Digital Lives"*

Professor Cal Newport, Georgetown University, *"Digital Minimalism – Choosing a Focused Life in a Noisy World"* and *"Deep Work: Rules for Focused Success in a Distracted World"* http://www.calnewport.com/

David Ryan Polgar, Esq., Pioneering Tech Ethicist and digital citizenship expert, co-host of *"Funny as Tech"* (podcast & live show), founder of *"All Tech Is Human,"* a collaborative, multi-disciplinary hub for more thoughtfulness around technology and the course, *"Digital Citizenship for Adults"* www.davidpolgar.com

Catherine Price, *"How to Break Up with Your Phone: The 30-Day Plan to Take Back Your Life"*

Douglas Rushkoff, Professor of Media Theory and Digital Economics at CUNY/Queens; author of *"Team Human," "Throwing Rocks at the Google Bus-How Growth Became the Enemy of Prosperity, Present Shock, "Program or Be Programmed—10 Commandments for a Digital Age," "Screenagers: Lessons in Chaos from Digital Kids"* https://rushkoff.com/

Professor Sherry Turkle, MIT, Abby Rockefeller Mauzé Professor of the Social Studies of Science and Technology, Founding Director, MIT Initiative on Technology and Self; *"Reclaiming Conversation: The Power of Talk in a Digital Age"* https://sherryturkle.com/

Dana Boyd, PhD, *"It's Complicated: The Social Lives of Networked Teens"* Data and Society, research institute on the social implications of data-centric technologies and automation (Microsoft supported); 2019 Electronic Frontier Foundation Award, http://www.danah.org/

Nir Eyal, *"Indistractable: How to Control Your Attention and Choose Your Life,"* originally expert in persuasive product design. https://www.nirandfar.com/

BJ Fogg, PhD, *"Tiny Habits – Small Changes That Change Everything,"* Behavior Scientist and expert in Persuasive Design, Stanford University, https://www.bjfogg.com/

Professor Tim Wu, Columbia Law School, *"The Attention Merchants – The Epic Scramble to Get Inside Our Heads"* http://www.timwu.org/

Professor Shoshana Zuboff, Harvard Business School, *"The Age of Surveillance Capitalism: The Fight for a Human Future at the New Frontier of Power"*

Manoush Zomorodi, *"Bored and Brilliant: How Spacing Out Can Unlock Your Most Productive and Creative Self."* http://www.manoushz.com/book

SELECT ARTICLES:

Internet Addiction Affects 6% of the World's Population, *Addiction.com*

https://www.addiction.com/3888/internet-addiction-worlds-population/

Are Teenagers Replacing Drugs With Smartphones?, *New York Times,* Matt Richtel

https://www.nytimes.com/2017/03/13/health/teenagers-drugs-smartphones.html

Record Numbers of College Students Are Seeking Treatment for Depression and Anxiety — But Schools Can't Keep Up, *Time Magazine*

https://time.com/5190291/anxiety-depression-college-university-students/

Mentions the American College Health Association survey of 63,000 students at 92 schools finding 40% of college students were so depressed in the prior year it was difficult to function and 61% "felt overwhelming anxiety" in the same time period.

Generation Z: Online and at Risk?, *Scientific American,* Nicholas Kardaras, PhD

https://www.scientificamerican.com/article/generation-z-online-and-at-risk/

Addicted to Screens?, *The New York Times, October 6, 2019*

https://www.nytimes.com/2019/10/06/technology/phone-screen-addiction-tech-nir-eyal.html

'Digital Addiction' a Real Threat to Kids?, *The New York Times*

https://www.nytimes.com/2019/05/20/well/family/is-digital-addiction-a-real-threat-to-kids.html

10 Ways to Protect the Brain from Daily Screen Time, *Psychology Today,* Victoria Dunckley, MD

https://www.psychologytoday.com/us/blog/mental-wealth/201704/10-ways-protect-the-brain-daily-screen-time

The Early Warning Signs of Screen Addiction, *Omega Recovery*

https://omegarecovery.org/the-early-warning-signs-of-screen-addiction/

Tech Diets Catch on With Apple Executives, Facebook Billionaires and Googlers

https://www.bloomberg.com/news/articles/2018-02-05/tech-diets-catch-on-with-apple-executives-facebook-billionaires-and-googlers

Is Your Child Overstimulated from Too Much Screen Time?, *Psychology Today,* Victoria Dunckley, MD https://www.psychologytoday.com/us/blog/mental-wealth/201711/is-your-child-overstimulated-too-much-screen-time

It's 'digital heroin': How screens turn kids into psychotic junkies, *New York Post,* Nicholas Kardaras, PhD, https://nypost.com/2016/08/27/its-digital-heroin-how-screens-turn-kids-into-psychotic-junkies/

Cal Newport on Why We'll Look Back at Our Smartphones Like Cigarettes,

GQ https://www.gq.com/story/cal-newport-digital-minimalism?verso=true

Steve Jobs Never Wanted Us to Use Our iPhones Like This, *New York Times,* The devices have become our constant companions. This was not the plan.

https://www.nytimes.com/2019/01/25/opinion/sunday/steve-jobs-never-wanted-us-to-use-our-iphones-like-this.html

Gray Matters: Too Much Screen Time Damages the Brain, *Psychology Today*, Victoria Dunckley, MD, https://www.psychologytoday.com/us/blog/mental-wealth/201402/gray-matters-too-much-screen-time-damages-the-brain

Screens In Schools Are a $60 Billion Hoax, *Time Magazine*, by Nicholas Kardaras, PhD

https://time.com/4474496/screens-schools-hoax/

Back-to-school: Time to set an electronic curfew,

Screenagers   https://www.screenagersmovie.com/tech-talk-tuesdays/back-to-school-time-to-set-an-electronic-curfew

"Tech Talk Tuesdays" Blog with *Screenagers* filmmaker and primary care physician, Delaney Ruston, MD, https://www.screenagersmovie.com/tech-talk-tuesdays

Is Your Smart Phone Making You Dumb? *Psychology Today*, Ron Friedman, PhD

https://www.psychologytoday.com/us/blog/glue/201501/is-your-smartphone-making-you-dumb

Have Smartphones Destroyed a Generation?, *The Atlantic*

https://www.theatlantic.com/magazine/archive/2017/09/has-the-smartphone-destroyed-a-generation/534198/

"Indistractable Review: Fixing Our Attention", *Wall Street Journal*, Belinda Lanks https://www.wsj.com/articles/indistractable-review-fixing-our-attention-11570142933

At Your Wits' End With A Screen-Obsessed Kid? Read This, *NPR* https://www.npr.org/2019/06/30/736214974/at-your-wits-end-with-a-screen-obsessed-kid-read-this?utm_campaign=storyshare&utm_source=twitter.com&utm_medium=social

Screentime Is Making Kids Moody, Crazy and Lazy, *Psychology Today,* Victoria Dunckley, MD

https://www.psychologytoday.com/us/blog/mental-wealth/201508/screentime-is-making-kids-moody-crazy-and-lazy

The Attention Diet

https://markmanson.net/attention-diet

Now Some Families Are Hiring Coaches to Help Them Raise Phone-Free Children, *The New York Times*

https://www.nytimes.com/2019/07/06/style/parenting-coaches-screen-time-phones.html

Nicholas Carr's dire warning: How technology is "making the world less interesting", *Salon*

https://www.salon.com/2014/12/24/nicholas_carrs_dire_warning_how_technology_is_making_the_world_less_interesting/

SELECT AUDIOS & VIDEOS:

AUDIO: NPR: 5 Strategies for Dealing with Screen-Obsessed Kids https://www.npr.org/2019/06/20/734532122/the-darker-side-of-screen-time

VIDEO: "Rethinking the Internet: How We Lost Control and How to Take It Back", May 3, 2019

https://www.youtube.com/watch?v=slsX_wihgCY

VIDEO: U.S. Senate Committee on Commerce, Science and Technology, Hearing on "Understanding the Use of Persuasive Technology on Internet Platforms", June 25, 2019

https://www.commerce.senate.gov/2019/6/optimizing-for-engagement-understanding-the-use-of-persuasive-technology-on-internet-platforms

VIDEO: The World Is Not the Screen, with Nicholas Carr

https://www.youtube.com/watch?v=CF9S0qSbV-s

VIDEO: Victoria Dunckley, MD on "Electronic Screen Syndrome"
https://www.youtube.com/watch?v=YM8LQ-bPEOE

VIDEO: Victoria Dunckley, MD on "The Overstimulated Child"

https://vimeo.com/132159417

VIDEO: The late Stanford University Professor Clifford Nass, PhD on multi-tasking risks, renowned expert on computer-human interaction

https://vimeo.com/78101118

VIDEO: "Tech Overuse and Addiction—What Can You Do?", NYC Manhattan Neighbors for Safer Telecommunications program, Fall 2018 https://manhattanneighbors.org/tech-addiction-oct-30-2018/

VIDEO: Joe Loizzo, MD, Weil Cornell Medical College & Columbia University Center for Buddhist Studies, on tech addiction: **"Diseases of Distraction and Opportunities for Healing"**.

https://vimeo.com/78725443

VIDEO: Angeles Arrien, PhD, Interview with cultural anthropologist Angeles Arrien, PhD by Camilla Rees, MBA of Manhattan Neighbors for Safer Telecommunications. https://vimeo.com/184519562

MOVIE: "WEB JUNKIE" China was the first country in the world to classify internet addiction as a clinical disorder and like some other Asian countries has hundreds of digital detox programs. WEB JUNKIE is focused on Internet Addiction, highlighting treatments used in Chinese Rehab Centers, including military-inspired physical training.

https://www.nytimes.com/2014/08/06/movies/web-junkie-examines-internet-addiction-in-china.html

VIDEO: "Doubling Down: Preserving Our Humanity in the Digital Age," Boston Museum of Science on March 26, 2019, with Jaron Lanier, Sue Halpern and Marcelo Gleiser

https://www.youtube.com/watch?v=8qpB9v-OrAU&feature=youtu.be

VIDEO: "Screen Addiction and Harm Occurring to Developing Children," Nicholas Kardaras, PhD, https://manhattanneighbors.org/kardaras/

VIDEO: "What You Need to Know About Internet Addiction" Dr. Kimberly Young, PsyD, Professor, St. Bonaventure University; Director, Center for Internet Addiction Recovery, https://www.youtube.com/watch?v=vOSYmLER664

AUDIO: CNET Book Club: Jaron Lanier on the future of VR and why we should all quit social media

https://www.cnet.com/news/cnet-book-club-episode-5-deleting-your-social-media-accounts-by-jaron-lanier/

OTHER RESOURCES

National Institute of Digital Health (www.USNIDH.org) New non-profit (501-c-3) that provides education, prevention and treatment resources for schools, families and therapists. Founded by Dr. Nicholas Kardaras, PhD.

Tristan Harris, Center for Humane Technology. Focused on reversing human downgrading and realigning technology with humanity. https://www.tristanharris.com/

Screenagers Professional Development in Schools. The "Screenagers" movie team is now offering a 6-hour, 3-part training module for professional development in schools. Contact Screenagers: www.screenagers.com

Paramount Wellness Institute, Health psychologist Brian Luke Seaward. Stress management expert, best-selling author, award winning documentary producer on Nature, corporate wellness consultant and stress management educator for Fortune 500 companies, the U.S. military, elite athletes, television personalities and actors, as well as educator on screen addiction and the human spirit, digital detox and mindfulness. https://www.brianlukeseaward.com/about/

Consciously Digital Consultancy (U.K.) with Anastasia Dedyukhina, PhD, author of *"Homo Distractus"*, helping people and organizations have healthier relationship with technology.

www.consciously-digital.com

Manhattan Neighbors for Safer Telecommunications. Education on the physical and mental health effects of modern technologies, including risks from cell phones, Wi-Fi, wireless computer equipment and technologies, excessive screen time, too early technology use, antennas in neighborhoods, etc., as well as on how to minimize tech risks in homes, offices and schools. www.manhattanneighbors.org

Screenagers: Growing Up in the Digital Age – Resources. Offer a range of valuable resources on subjects ranging from internet addiction to school cell phone policies, screen time contracts, bullying, sleep and screens, etc. https://www.screenagersmovie.com/resources-2

Building Biology Institute. Trains the general public and working professionals (architects, builders, engineers, interior designers, physicians, nurses, and other health care practitioners, real estate professionals, environmental consultants, etc.) on how to create healthy homes, schools and workplaces free of indoor air and tap water pollution and hazards posed by computers, and other electronic equipment, if not hard-wired. Referral list. www.buildingbiologyinstitute.org

Common Sense Media. A leading advisor on media and technology focused on families and schools. Research impact of media and tech use on children's physical, emotional, social, and intellectual development. Also, have focus on children's privacy and digital citizenry. Advise on movies and tv.

https://www.commonsensemedia.org

*The author of this book does not necessarily endorse the worldviews, philosophies, or political views of the authors listed above. The books, articles, and films stand on their own merit either because of or despite the views of their authors.

ENDNOTES

1   https://www.techwalla.com/articles/the-purpose-of-the-cell-phone
2   https://mobilecoach.com/8-surprising-cell-phone-statistics/
3   https://www.zmescience.com/science/news-science/smartphone-power-compared-to-apollo-432/
4   Hawkins, David R., Power vs. Force. Hay House Publishers, 1995. P. XXXIX
5   Matthew 7:24-27 NIV
6   https://en.wikipedia.org/wiki/Luddite
7   Genesis 3:1 NIV
8   https://www.theneurotypical.com/psychological_coercion.html
9   https://www.theguardian.com/us-news/2019/may/15/camp-fire-pge-cause-calfire
10 https://www.cdc.gov/tobacco/data_statistics/fact_sheets/youth_data/movies/index.htm
11 https://www.gamesradar.com/video-games-and-the-dark-art-of-seducing-players/
12 https://www.researchgate.net/publication/329819896_Technological_Seduction_and_Self-Radicalization
13 https://www.healthline.com/health/mental-health/cell-phone-addiction#about-phone-addiction
14 https://www.psychiatry.org/patients-families/addiction/what-is-addiction
15 Damon Zahariades, *Digital Detox: The Ultimate guide to Beating Technology Addiction, Cultivating Mindfulness, and Enjoying More Creativity, Inspiration, and Balance in Your Life!* http://artofproductivity.com/my-books/
16 https://www.psychologytoday.com/us/basics/dopamine
17 IBID
18 https://www.youtube.com/watch?v=l2tZLesCX4M
19 1 Peter 3:15
20 https://www.guardchild.com/social-media-statistics-2/#:~:text=Social%20Media%20Statistics,frequently%E2%80%9D%20on%20social%20networking%20sites.
21 https://internetsafety101.org/cyberbullyingstatistics

22 https://www.kait8.com/story/38433832

23 Proverbs 23:7, Luke 12:21

24 Ephesians 5:16

25 https://www.webmd.com/mental-health/addiction/news/20091006/internet-addiction-is-your-teen-at-risk

26 Mary Pipher, *The Shelter of Each Other*. Random House, Inc., New York, 1996. (Thirsty in the Rain chapter).

27 Proverbs 8:12

28 Proverbs 27:12

29 https://www.livescience.com/22281

30 Ibid.

31 https://faculty.washington.edu/chudler/inskull.html

32 https://faculty.washington.edu/chudler/inskull.html

33 Philippians 4:8 NIV

34 https://www.desiringgod.org/articles/where-is-jesus-in-the-old-testament

35 Colossians 4:5

36 John 9:4

37 James 2:18

38 Romans 13:11

39 Ephesians 5:15-17

40 Proverbs 6:10-11

41 Ecclesiastes 3:17

42 Proverbs 27:1

43 Mary Pipher, page 18.

44 Acts 17:26

45 Psalm 16:5-9

46 Psalm 136: 8-9

47 Job 38:10-11

48 Proverbs 8:29

49 https://www.adweek.com/brand-marketing/throwback-thursday-when-doctors-prescribed-healthy-cigarette-brands-165404/#:~:text=Don't%20be%20foolish%2C%20take,they%20still%20made%20smokers%20cough.

50 https://www.webmd.com/depression/news/20100802/internet-overuse-may-cause-depression#:~:text=Aug.,users%2C%20a%20new%20study%20says.

51 https://www.webmd.com/parenting/features/4-dangers-internet#4

52 https://www.webmd.com/mental-health/news/20041202/death-hyperlink-internet-suicide-pacts#2

53 https://www.webmd.com/parenting/features/4-dangers-internet#1

54 Luke 6:48-49

55 Ibid.

56 Galatians 5:22-23

57 https://www.josh.org/9-important-insights-generation-z/?mwm_id=263463
299518&mot=J79GNF&gclid=CjwKCAjwjqT5BRAPEiwAJlBuBbjYSMJ
2klMgvf6Wu3NU2UhRK5S6IZQWdIgz3X9VAYeUW2DkD509NhoCz
foQAvD_BwE

58 https://review42.com/how-much-time-do-people-spend-on-social-media/

59 https://www.google.com/search?q=How+many+kids+watch+YouTube&oq=H
ow+many+kids+watch+YouTube&aqs=chrome..69i57.5021j1j7&sourceid=
chrome&ie=UTF-8

60 https://www.ncbi.nlm.nih.gov/pmc/articles/PMC6706260/

61 Gordon Livingston, *Too Soon Old, Too Late Smart.* (Philadelphia, PA: Da Capo
Press, 2004).

62 IBID.

63 Bernadette Noll, *Slow Family Living.* (New York: PERIGEE/Penguin Books,
2013).

64 IBID.

65 IBID.

66 Love, T., Laier, C., Brand, M., Hatch, L., & Hajela, R. (2015). Neuroscience of
internet pornography addiction: A Review and update. *Behavioral Sciences,* (5),
388-423.

67 https://thedoctorweighsin.com/why-is-pornography-so-powerfully-
addictive/#:~:text=The%20simple%20answer%20is%20that,the%20
neuroscience%20of%20internet%20pornography.

68 IBID.

69 https://www.bbc.co.uk/bitesize/guides/z897pbk/revision/2

70 https://en.wikipedia.org/wiki/Greta_Thunberg

71 °

72 https://pubmed.ncbi.nlm.nih.gov/23863754/

73 https://www.webmd.com/sleep-disorders/sleep-blue-light#:~:text=Exposure%20
to%20all%20colors%20of,melatonin%20that%20makes%20you%20sleepy.

74 https://abcdstudy.org/

75 https://www.forbes.com/sites/nextavenue/2017/01/04/try-the-30-day-digital-
detox-challenge/#3f2f37b93a3d

76 Colier, Nancy. *The Power of Off: The Mindful Way to Stay Sane in a Virtual
World.* Boulder, CO, Sounds True, Inc., 2016. [Used with permission from the
author]

77 Romans 12:10 NIV

78 https://www.statista.com/statistics/189959/housing-units-with-telephones-
in-the-united-states-since-1920/

79 http://www.classicrotaryphones.com/useit1.html

80 https://digital.hagley.org/20120418_How_To_Make_Friends#page/5/mode/1up

81   Robert Fulghum, *All I Really Need to Know I Learned in Kindergarten*. New York, Random House Publishers, 1986.

82   IBID.

83   https://drpfconsults.com/4-real-reasons-why-teachers-leave-the-profession/

84   https://www.businessinsider.com/talking-on-a-hands-free-cellphone-is-as-bad-as-driving-drunk-2013-8#:~:text=The%20available%20studies%20so%20far,or%20worse%20than%20driving%20drunk.&text=This%20year%2C%20a%20study%20at,cellphone%20drivers%20was%20roughly%20equal.

85   Proverbs 22:6

86   Christian Lous Lange

87   Psalm 111:10

88   Philippians 4:8

89   Richard Lou, *Last Child in the Woods*. (New York: Workman Publishing, 2005, 2008).

90   https://www.ewg.org/sunscreen/report/the-trouble-with-sunscreen-chemicals/

91   https://www.cga.ct.gov/2013/rpt/2013-R-0329.htm

92   https://chadd.org/adhd-weekly/spend-time-outside-to-improve-adhd-symptoms/#:~:text=A%20growing%20body%20of%20research,children%20with%20an%20ADHD%20diagnosis.

93   https://www.bupa.co.uk/newsroom/ourviews/teenager-loneliness#:~:text=40%20percent%20of%2016%20to,felt%20lonely%20than%20older%20children.

94   https://time.com/5833681/loneliness-covid-19/

95   https://time.com/5833681/loneliness-covid-19/

96   IBID

97   https://images.search.yahoo.com/search/images;_ylt=AwrE19zqD2xf9GYAJThXNyoA;_ylu=Y29sbwNiZjEEcG9zAzQEdnRpZAMEc2VjA3Nj?p=wrecking+ball+miley+cyrus&fr=mcafee

98   https://www.simpletoremember.com/articles/a/dangers-of-television/

99   IBID

100 1 Corinthians 13:12

101 Mario Murillo

102 Carolyne Myss, *Intimate Conversations with the Divine*, Hay House, Inc. 2020.

103 https://video.search.yahoo.com/search/video?fr=mcafee&p=billy+crystal+lines+from+city+slickers#id=52&vid=cf95e9b61f69f019bfd889729067ca4b&action=click

104 John 17:15

105 Zechariah 4:6